NEIL

To a brave BA Captain
Hope you enjoy the
read.   John K

OBSERVATIONS FROM THE TOWER

First published in 2003 by

WOODFIELD PUBLISHING
Bognor Regis, West Sussex, England
www.woodfieldpublishing.com

© John Kilburn, 2003

The right of John Kilburn
to be identified as Author of this work
has been asserted in accordance with
the Copyright, Designs and Patents Act 1988

ISBN 1-903953-43-X

Observations from the Tower

MEMOIRS OF A FORMER AIR TRAFFIC CONTROLLER

John Kilburn

Woodfield

I dedicate this book in the first instance to my late beloved wife Bette, my son Howard, daughter Wendy & grandson Richard (all, of whom appear in the narrative) for the support and encouragement they gave me whilst I was putting pen to paper.

Secondly to all the friends and colleagues with whom I worked during my years as an Air Traffic Controller.

Blackpool's 'other' tower and my 'home from home' for over 30 years.

The Author at work in the 'Ivory Tower'.

Contents

FOREWORD

The UK Aviation scene has changed beyond recognition during the past few years. Travellers have witnessed the amazing growth of the low cost airlines and along with every other industry, aviation has witnessed 'an invasion' by computer technology. There has also been an insidious growth in bureaucracy largely associated with the litigation culture, which is so prevalent in the western world today. So there is much more paperwork and an increased reliance on the rulebook. The reader could be forgiven for thinking that following the rule book is no bad thing, but as in many aspects of life, the rules, if followed to the letter, actually slow down the traffic flow.

It has been said that rules are there for the guidance of wise men and the blind obedience of idiots. John Kilburn was in the wise men category. He was, in old-fashioned parlance, a first class seat of the pants controller. As he describes in this volume, John knew the rulebook. That had been drilled in during his training. More importantly he knew when to throw the rulebook out of the window and, using his vast experience, make decisions, which enabled traffic to flow, in the words of the ATC bible, 'safely and expeditiously'.

I had the pleasure of working with the author during his final five years in aviation. He was a first class, dependable and professional operator. For John those final few years were a hobby for which he was paid. I think he would have worked just for the pleasure of it but perhaps his Yorkshire born wife would have insisted that 'tha doesn't do owt for nowt!'

You see John was one of the last real characters in UK ATC. He was passionate about aviation and had grown up with the embryo civil aviation industry, which 'took off' after the hostilities of the Second World War. In those days the rules were made up as you went along. In John's early days in ATC, equipment was very basic and the ability to use initiative and common sense was an over riding primary requirement. So you can see that all this was a world away from the ATC system, which John left on his final retirement.

So I think that John left the industry at the right time. A lot of the fun had gone out of the job. A new breed of controllers with little or no passion for aviation has largely replaced the characters who manned our ATC units in years gone by.

This book is a fascinating read about those foundation days of civil aviation in which John Kilburn and his contemporaries played such an important part. I am delighted that John has seen his recollections in print and along with many of his former colleagues I wish John a continued long and happy retirement.

David Edmondson, 2003

ACKNOWLEDGEMENTS

To the following individuals I extend my warmest thanks for contributing items, suggestions, anecdotes, etc where my memory failed me. Also those persons, few in number, who having read the MSS persuaded me that a publisher might well be interested.

- Stan Lynch CAA SRG (ATC Inspector) for suggesting the project in the first place.
- Richard (my grandson) for suggesting an apt title for the book.
- Gill Whaite (ATCO) for word processing the entire MSS in a presentable format.
- Peter & Barbara Houghton (ex ATCO & ATCA respectively) Pete was my deputy for the majority of the 16 years I was the SATCO and thus his considerable input into my story.
- Corey Turner (ex ATCO)
- John Halliwell - Co. Air Pageant organiser & aviation enthusiast.
- Sid Grant - Ex businessman & Private pilot.
- Alwyn Evans - Marine pilot.
- Any others I may have missed out. I apologise in advance.

Finally I am particularly indebted to the following two gentleman for encouraging me to pursue publishing potential.

- Firstly DAVE EDMONDSON (my Boss and the SATCO upon my retirement) who undertook the not inconsiderable task of completely editing & updating the manuscript into computer format. His comments in his foreword (unsolicited) speak for themselves.
- Secondly Clive McKrell (an ex-controller colleague) who upon reading my mss headed his own (again unsolicited appraisal of my efforts with just three words… "Get it Published"!

The Author in uniform as a Civil Aviation Radio Officer.

INTRODUCTION

A 'Life Sentence' in Aviation 1943 – 1995

I finally hung up my electric hat as an Air Traffic Control Officer having spent over half a century in the aviation environment, 38 years of which, apart from one interval, were spent in Air Traffic Control; on reflection, not a bad innings, considering I ended my career with an unblemished record of service. But how did it all start? My involvement can best be summarised by as follows:

1.	R.A.F. Aircrew	Signaller	1943 – 1947
2.	Civil Aircrew	Radio Officer	1948 – 1957
3.	Air Traffic Control	Air Traffic Controller	1957– 1995

As the last phase was by far the longest time I had spent in any of the above professions, it is this part of my career that constitutes the bulk of my memoirs. However, I cannot, ignore phase one and two, as, without them, I doubt whether I would have considered Air Traffic Control as a career in the first place.

One might ask who had suggested that my memoirs might be worth putting into print. Ironically, it was a Civil Aviation Authority (CAA) Examiner who, having brought my career to a close, suggested this idea as a retirement project. He was of the opinion that a readership market would be interested in my experiences; for instance, comparing my era of controlling with modern day methods.

Frankly I was surprised at his suggestion, said in all seriousness. To my way of thinking publishers only considered manuscripts such as I was contemplating if written by persons known to the public at large. For example World War two service persons with a string of medals to their name or, prominent people such as politicians, etc., who had interesting stories to tell?

By contrast, I am purely a non-descript aviation person having no claim to fame, but, with the encouragement of my erstwhile benefactor, it is just conceivable he might have a point. Hence the reason I am taking his advice.

The curtailment of my career was as a direct result of reaching the ripe old age of three score years and ten and, accepting the irreversible fact that Anno Domini had set in. The powers to be obviously thought I had had enough. I must admit that my thought processes were possibly on the decline so, better to leave with an untarnished reputation rather than be cast aside as a 'has-been'.

When one considers that controllers employed by the National Air Traffic Services, by far the largest employer of such personnel, are automatically retired at the age of sixty (I was local government employed), I consider my extension of employment, beyond the norm, was stretching my luck, but it held! My extended service was due to a shortage of qualified controllers at the time. Somewhere along the line I must have created a favourable impression! At least I achieved my ambition of being an operational controller by the time I reached my seventieth birthday. Incidentally, the year before, I had written an article which was published in the CAA newsletter 'Airway' enquiring if any other controller could match my performance, relative to my age. I had a sneaking suspicion that I may have been the oldest operational controller in the U.K. Only one person challenged my claim. I discovered though that the aerodrome he worked at, only operated an Aerodrome Flight Information Service (A.F.I.S..) which is a lesser qualification than the full ATC service I was providing. Maybe then, my claim was valid after all!

Before I start writing my story, is it not a fact that a lot of people, if they are honest, would like to see themselves in print? Therefore, being of similar persuasion, if I am lucky enough to find an interested publisher, the time and effort I have spent in relating my life's work, will not have been in vain. Being a realist though, my scribings are more likely to end up under the heading of "and what did you do with your life granddad"?

At least my grandchildren will appreciate my efforts – I hope!

1   My Formative Years

Traditionally most autobiographies initially describe one's youth in detail, no doubt to paint a characteristic picture of why that particular person made an outstanding success of their subsequent life. I confess though, when reading such tomes, I find these particular aspects of a persons life can be a bit of a bore, consequently I cannot wait to read on and go to the heart of the individual achievements.

This is where I now intend to break with tradition and only describe my formative years very briefly. I am helped in this deliberate ploy by an honest lack of memory and those people, my foster family who brought me up, who could elaborate on such matters, they having long departed these shores. They live in Canada now, although we still keep in touch regularly.

At the tender age of four, my Mother and Father deposited me with a family, used to fostering children whose parents are otherwise committed. They went to Australia on holiday. Why I did not go with them, I have no idea. Maybe the encumbrance of a small child was not conductive to a relaxed vacation! I subsequently learnt that my parents were not very parentally minded anyway. On their return from Australia they parted company. Mother returned to her beloved London (I was born in Hendon) and father to his equally beloved Scotland, Edinburgh to be precise. Consequently my foster parents, the Henderson's, brought me up as though I was one of their family. They had three daughters and a son of similar age to myself. Our upbringing was conventional and mainly a happy one, albeit tempered at times by a rather strict head of the family. He was a former World War 1 Army Officer with Victorian ideas on family rearing, and discipline. In later years, some of his principles would stand me in good stead when I had a family of my own. Lets face it, bringing up children to be well mannered, and show respect to their elders is one of the hardest tasks in life. Therefore part of the Henderson's example was a useful yardstick to go by. For that reason, and others, I was grateful for the circumstances under which I found myself during my formative years.

From the age of nine, right up to my eighteenth birthday, my education was conducted in boarding schools. On reflection, I was not enamoured with this type of schooling. Nowadays, co-education in such establishments is becoming the norm whereas, in my day, the norm was single sex pupils only. It is the latter aspect that I am against. Co-ed pupils, particularly in boarding schools are, in my opinion, ensconced in a more healthy environment in which to learn the three R's. Why did I end up in boarding schools rather than day schools attendance as enjoyed by my foster parent's children? This is where my own Mother, in the first instance, and my Godfather, a certain Sir Harry Peat of a well-known London firm of Accountants, in the second place, decided my educational life-style. I attended Dane Court Prep: school in Byfleet Surrey, and Bryanston Public School in Blandford Dorset. It was the latter school that my Godfather was insistent that I attend. As he paid the fees etc., I had no choice in the matter. Quite frankly, he need not have bothered, as I was NOT a bright pupil. In fact I didn't even pass the School Certificate Examination. Digressing for a moment, a word or two about this particular Public School is, I think worth a comment if, for no other reason than it was considered a rather progressive establishment, compared to the accepted image of such schools. For example, our uniform was novel to say the least. Bearing in mind that the majority of us did not leave until we were eighteen years of age, our attire consisted of short trousers, knee length woolen stockings, and matching shirt and pullover – all in a delicate shade of bluey grey! We didn't even have blazers.

Apart from holiday time, I didn't get into wearing long trousers, on a permanent basis, until I joined the R.A.F.

Another 'novelty' was their own version of Chinese Torture to wake us up in the morning. We were required, Summer and Winter, to completely immerse ourselves in a bath of stone cold water – in and out smartish – followed by a quick dress to run round the block; and all before breakfast! Whether this treatment paid dividends in the long run is hard to say. Possibly I can attribute my present health and well being, at the ripe old age of seventy-two as I write this, to this form of treatment.

It was at Bryanston that I first experienced wartime dangers. The school building was a prominent pre-war mansion situated in an elevated position. I believe a certain Lord Portman once owned it. Anyway, on one particularly brilliant moonlit night a German bomber, no doubt thinking our school was some sort of military HQ, bearing all the hallmarks of such an establishment, decided we were a worthwhile target and promptly off-loaded his bombs upon us. Fortunately he missed; all his 'eggs' fell onto the school grounds, some of which didn't even explode. The following morning I can well remember my feelings. I thought our days were numbered and the future filled me with awe.

On another occasion, whilst playing rugby one afternoon, all of a sudden there was the unmistakable sound of a machine-gun fire. Sure enough, not more than half a mile away a German bomber – a Dornier 17, more commonly known as the 'flying pencil' – was being hotly pursued by a Hurricane fighter. The bomber ended up in a belly-crash landing, whilst the fighter did a victory roll over our heads.

Some might say "what a way to remember one's school days"! Be that as it may, these short recollections tend to make up for my lack of scholastic achievements, mentioned earlier.

As I spent most of my youth tucked away in boarding schools the only time I could enjoy a normal family life was during holiday time but I have to admit, it doesn't seem to have done me any harm.

In the latter part of my teens and, in particular, after I had come out of the R.A.F., revelations about my Mother and Father's background, not to mention my half-brother and half-sister (same mother, different father) came to light. Mother was an artist, a Portrait Miniaturist who, incidentally, exhibited in the Royal Academy every year, even into her late seventies. Because of her talents, she was also a member of the Royal Society of Miniature Painters. Father, who I never really knew, was, from all accounts, a brilliant engineer. I was told he was head of the BSA works during World War One. Subsequently he, in conjunction with a financier colleague, started up an automobile firm by the name of SHAW & KILBURN. They were franchised dealers for Vauxhall and Bedford trucks. I believe they were still in existence till quite recently. I was also told that, at one time, he must have been very wealthy. He had a mansion adjacent to a Scottish Loch (I never did discover the location) the grounds of which were so large that he had a miniature steam train running through them. He also had his own motor launch on the nearby loch. As proof of what I was told, my mother gave me some photographs of father's material wealth, one of which depicts me as a baby, sitting on the engine's tender. Sad to relate that due to circumstances that were never divulged he eventually lost the lot; and to think I might have inherited his stately 'pile' with all its goodies!

Gill, my half sister was, like mother, an artist. Amongst her achievements she was responsible for London's annual Regent Street Christmas decorations. She also became a titled lady by her second marriage to Labour MP Tony Greenwood (son of the wartime cabinet minister, Arthur Greenwood). Tony was elevated to the peerage upon the dissolution of the then Labour Government.

Rupert, my half brother (both he and Gill were considerably older than me) was a philosopher and wrote books on the subject. He was a great friend of the well-known philosopher Bertrand Russell.

As an indication of how disjointed a family we were… some time ago my own family and I attended a party in London, which turned out to be a gathering of the Huxley Clan (more of my connection with this illustrious family in a moment). Rupert, on being told that his brother – me – was at this party, promptly denied all knowledge of my existence. I, at least, was aware of his presence albeit that to the best of my knowledge, we had never previously met. The upshot of this unusual state of affairs was that we were introduced to each other! A novel way of finding out who one was related to.

Gill did at least keep in partial contact with me until I blotted my copybook. I was staying with her at her Hampstead home while studying for my civil flying licence. Due to being married to a Labour MP she had become an ardent socialist and tried to persuade me to go down the mines as a 'Bevin Boy' – the in-thing to do at this point in the history of the Labour government. Despite my having served in the R.A.F., Gill apparently thought I was 'malingering' as a student. Not unnaturally we parted company. I returned to Mother to continue with my studies. At this stage of my life the Hendersons had moved to Torquay, hence the reason I was staying with Gill in London, it being nearer to the aviation scene to enter the profession I had opted for.

At about the time I found out more about my immediate family further revelations were forthcoming. On mother's side, it transpired we were well connected and could claim so called 'Upper Class' status in society; our heritage was such that we appeared to have 'Blue Blood' running through our veins.

The Huxley family were very much at the forefront of these connections. Indeed, some years ago, a book was written exclusively about them which, amongst other things, a family tree was incorporated including yours truly, who appeared as a small twig on one of the tree's branches. We even appear in the aristocrat's bible – *De Bretts Peerage & Baronetage*. A full page insert in this book is headed by a certain Baron Monkswell, who started it all. It wouldn't be truthful if I did not admit that I am proud of the fact that my own family, wife Bette, son Howard and daughter Wendy are also included.

Postscript

After I had penned this part of my manuscript I discovered some more interesting details about my father. In the past I really hadn't taken much notice of my parents' background, in fact, it wasn't until I was in my early seventies that I started to take an interest.

My Rotary Air Display co-organiser John Halliwell was a railway enthusiast and consequently took an interest in my father's miniature railway. He contacted a similar enthusiast – a certain Peter Scott – who, it transpired, is a noted authority on all matters relating to miniature trains; he even writes articles on his researches on such matters. Come to think of it, I suppose I should have done more in the research department in the first place! Anyway, the upshot of these enquiries revealed that, contrary to what I had been led to believe, my father's miniature railway was at his home in Hendon London, my birthplace (as witnessed by digging up my long forgotten birth certificate).

That was one mystery of my family background resolved, although I'm still puzzled about father's motor launch! I'm not aware of any Lochs in the vicinity of Hendon! The photographs I have of his boat all indicate a typical Scottish scenic background.

On a recent visit to the R.A.F. Museum in Hendon I located my birthplace, which is now a collection of warden controlled old people's homes. I spoke to one of the female wardens who confirmed that the place was once a private residence but she had no recollection of a miniature railway running around the garden. The present day complex still retains its original title, Derby House, as written on my birth certificate.

2 OH, WHAT A LOVELY WAR – 1943-47

Two weeks after leaving school I was in the R.A.F. What prompted this rapid transformation of my lifestyle? It must be remembered this was wartime. I had no intention of being conscripted into the armed forces, which would have been my lot if I hadn't volunteered.

At school I was in the Air Training Corps Squadron, in which I seemed reasonably proficient in Wireless Telegraphy – in particular Morse code – so, I thought, why not volunteer for R.A.F. aircrew as a WOP/AG (air Gunner). This aircrew trade was eventually separated into two categories, namely WOP/AIR and AG. I chose the former. Strangely enough, I had no desire to become a pilot, which was just as well as, academically speaking; I would not have qualified anyway.

I had never flown in my life and, consequently, knew little or nothing about aeroplanes except what I had learnt about them whilst in the ATC.

The only distinction I managed as an ATC cadet was winning a competition on the subject of equivalent ranks in the Navy, Army and Air Force. For my efforts, I received a book about the R.A.F., presented to me by our Commanding Officer. I still have this book today.

The thought of flying did not particularly bother me. I suppose I was more interested in the 'glamour' of the uniform I hoped to wear, if I made the grade. I refer of course to the coveted flying brevet and badges of rank. Little did I realise at the time what I would have to cope with to reach such status?

Having successfully passed the entrance examinations and the aircrew medical board – this being a stringent in-depth examination of one's bodily functions – I was committed and henceforth, sallied forth into the unknown.

I can recall to this day my thoughts as I entered LORDS cricket ground, which was the Aircrew Reception Centre (ACRC) for prospective aircrew cadets. "I shall never be a free person again, service life will rule for evermore"!

My co-volunteers and I were housed in a block of flats situated behind this famous cricket ground. Our stay was long enough to be kitted out, enjoy the delights of 'square bashing' and, worst of all, being jabbed right left and centre by the medics; presumably to ward off any nasty diseases we might contract throughout our service life.

As I had spent the majority of my youth cooped up in boarding schools, I did not suffer the pangs of homesickness that some poor unfortunate beings did, they having come straight from a home environment. Having said that, although I was not over enamoured with life at boarding school, at least the experience stood me in good stead for a relatively smooth transition to service life.

Initial Training Wing (ITW)

This establishment attempted to make us motley u/t aircrew into disciplined service men, capable of holding our own with our brothers in arms, in the other two services. I fear our instructors must have felt it was an uphill struggle at times! They tried hard to instil a sense of pride in our chosen service. We became embroiled in endless parade ground drills, physical exercises (PE), and sundry other activities, all designed to mould us into responsible airmen. At this stage there appeared to be little or no connection with flying in aeroplanes!

On arrival at this camp, I can well remember our introduction to the NCO who would be in charge of our squad throughout our stay. He was a former Guards Sergeant who had transferred to the R.A.F., retaining his rank. To give him his due, although a strict disciplinarian, he was fair when dealing with the more unruly elements among us. His first task was to teach us how to polish one's boots. Low and behold, he took one of mine and polished it so well, in true guardsman fashion that, for evermore, it outshone my other boot! I could never match his expertise. In one respect I was the envy of my colleagues but on the other hand, the butt of many snide remarks about not being able to 'shoe-shine' my other boot in the prescribed manner. Square bashing, as I have said, was our main pre-occupation which, incidentally, I must have got the hang of, as I was awarded a white lanyard (equivalent to the rank of corporal) enabling me to occasionally issue parade ground orders, rather than being on the receiving end.

Amongst our other attention seekers was the usage of different firearms, and lectures on just about every facet of life in the R.A.F. One aspect of the latter was the question of National Security, a very necessary part of our service education. Posters entitled 'Careless talk costs lives' were everywhere but, it was the dire consequences of what could happen to us, if we ignored the implications, that put the fear of god in me!

I enjoyed the firearm exercises, especially the Sten gun and Clay Pigeon shooting details. The standard.303 rifle was a different matter. It took quite a bit of getting used to because of the kick it gave when you fired it.

A novel institution, on the catering side, is worth a mention. Our mugs of tea were regularly laced with Bromide. This was supposed to curb any amorous desires we might have which, if unchecked, could deter us from paying attention to what our Lords and Masters wanted us to learn, and inwardly digest. I am not sure it was entirely successful the R.A.F.'s way of curbing our natural instincts!

As I am relying upon memory, it is difficult to relate any other things of note that happened whilst at ITW. So, rather than bore whoever reads this saga with unnecessary comments, I might as well move on to the next stage of my training whereby I became more involved in real live aeroplanes – my first acquaintance with them since joining up.

Radio School – Yatesbury

At this camp, most of our time initially, was spent in the class room getting to know different types of radio gear carried in aircraft i.e. transmitters and receivers, and their associated bits and pieces. Use of the Morse key, sending and receiving messages, working up the speed of transmissions, 25 words per minute being the target to aim for. All sounds very simple when one describes such activities in few words but there was a lot of ground to cover hence the longevity of this course. I forgot its duration; suffice to say it was in the order of months rather than weeks.

In between ground lectures, classroom exercises were put to the test in the air, at regular intervals. The object being a) to get us used to being airborne and, b) carry out simple transmit and receive exercises on the aircraft's radio equipment. Yatesbury had its own grass airfield. There were two types of aircraft used to train us, namely the DH Rapide and the Percival Proctor.

On my first flight I will never forget what 'Terra Firma' looked like from an aeroplane. Buildings, people, vehicles etc, all in miniature, and the surrounding countryside like a patchwork quilt, albeit not multi-coloured, as one usually associates with this term; more greens and browns than anything else. A fascinating experience to a sprog aviator and, I am glad to say, no sign of airsickness.

Initially we flew the Rapides, about six cadets at a time, until we were judged proficient enough to operate solo on the Proctor; just the pilot and oneself. Before we started flying, we were kitted up with all the flying gear we were liable to wear in the future. If one donned the lot, you could be mistaken for the 'Michelin Man' particularly if you were big made – fortunately I wasn't.

During our time at this camp, square bashing, PE, weapons drill, etc, was not forgotten. Even spells of night guard duties had to be contended with; not a very pleasant chore, especially during the winter months.

Whilst on the subject of extra curricula duties, an alarming experience occurred one day whilst on the firing range, which incorporated a parapet slit trench for grenade throwing practice. We were, on this particular occasion, throwing LIVE hand grenades, the objective being to lob them over the parapet, for obvious reasons. The inevitable happened as one of our colleagues, small in stature, failed to clear the parapet, whereupon the grenade stuck fast atop. I have never seen grown men scarper so fast in all their lives before the device exploded; there was earth and debris everywhere! At the time we were not amused but, on reflection, it was hilarious to see the antics we got up to in avoiding a dangerous situation. On a lighter note, I ought to point out that our life-style was not all work and no play. Aircrews are not noted for taking life too seriously except when duty calls. Socialising was mainly confined to the camp NAAFI. Most of the time we were too knackered to venture further afield. Occasionally though, pastures new DID beckon us. The nearest built-up area was the nearby town of CALNE. What the locals thought of all us young 'boys in blue', parading through their domain and occasionally causing mayhem, I hate to think. It was here that I first sampled the delights of alcoholic beverages. I had already succumbed to nicotine so, to complete my manhood, this was the logical step forward to fulfil my 'coming of age'; in other words, be one of the lads. To say I disgraced myself would be putting it mildly. I got 'blotto' on one pint of beer. I had to be carried back to camp, fortunately without being apprehended by the ever vigilant service police (SP's). By a gradual process I built up my intake so that I could hold my own with the majority of them. I never became a hardened drinker though.

In due course, the all-important day arrived whereby we were assembled, en masse, and presented with our brevets and sergeant's stripes. We had made the grade so far and, unashamedly strutted about showing off our sergeant's tapes and sporting our wings. No longer 'wingless wonders', as we tended to irreverently describe our non-aircrew brethren. The rush to find tailors, invariably WAAFS we had befriended, who were prepared to adorn our uniforms with our newly won insignias, was quite an exercise in itself.

After the graduation ceremony, we were packed off on leave to await postings to the next stage of our flying career. Not a bit of it though, as well we all found ourselves back at Yatesbury. Unbeknown to us there was, all of a sudden, a glut of Wireless Operators, which meant a delay in getting us away to the next stage of our training, The Advanced Flying Unit (AFU). So, here we were, all two thousand of us with nowhere to go. The inevitable happened, we did the whole course again and, to add insult to injury, we were required to wear the white flash in our forage caps (the insignia denoting u/t aircrew before being awarded their wings), an order that had never, to my knowledge, been invoked before. With hindsight, this delay in our training schedule was to prove fortuitous, as witness the title I have given in describing my R.A.F. career.

After Yatesbury and before proceeding to my first AFU, for some inexplicable reason I found myself, alone, dispatched to Marshall's Field Cambridge. For three weeks I languished in this establishment, as a newly qualified aircrew bod, with nothing to do but amuse myself as best I could. I do not recall anyone else of my status being posted to such a place, particularly as it did not cater for the type of training – AFU – I should be undertaking.

The powers to be eventually woke up to the fact that they had put a square peg into a round hole – me – and, without further ado, posted me back into the training programme where I should have gone in the first place.

Ironically I was destined to attend not one but two AFU's. The first one was Moreton Valence (near Gloucester), the second being Llandwrog (North Wales) now, incidentally Caernavon civil airport. Both units operated Anson aircraft. I can only conclude that the reason for a double dose of AFU's was due to the snarl up in our training schedule, which first became apparent at our prolonged sojourn at Yatesbury. I hasten to add, if only to have a clear conscience, that these delaying tactics were beyond my control.

Amazing as it might seem, I have little recollection of my flying participation whilst in the R.A.F., even to the extent that I have to refer to my log book to convince myself that I did, indeed, fly with the R.A.F.!

The only thing that sticks out in my mind whilst at these AFU's is a certain episode that happened whilst attending the second one – Llandwrog. One-weekend volunteers were asked to undertake a rather morbid task. A few days previously an Anson aircraft (not one of ours) with four Flight Lieutenants on board, had crashed in the mountains, not far from our airfield. Digressing for a moment, a lot of our flying was uncomfortably close to mountainous terrain. Anyway, back to the matter in hand. Our task was to locate the crashed aircraft and, if necessary, retrieve the bodies from the wreckage. Being young and naïve and, some would say, bloody fools a few of us offered our services. What stuck in my mind was first that I had never seen a dead body before and second, when a colleague and I lifted one of the dead airmen to put the body on a stretcher, it broke in half! And what did we have for lunch afterwards – corn beef sandwiches!

I suppose the reason why such events did not really affect us too much, was our naivety, and acceptance, that such tragedies were inevitable during wartime. On a more pleasant note, the billets we occupied at this camp were situated on a shingle beach right on the shore of Caernavon Bay. A delightful setting for our stay at this camp and, set far enough from the airfield itself, necessitating a bus service every time we went flying. Many years later, on a nostalgic trip, I revisited this site; the remnants of our billets were still to be seen.

From AFU to O.T.U

Here again the powers to be posted me to, not one, but two O.T.U's (operational training units). At this stage of my service life, I seemed destined to attend each stage of my training in duplicate; Noah's Ark and the animals comes to mind!

My introduction to the first O.T.U to which I had been posted, Lossiemouth in Scotland, was not exactly encouraging. On the night I arrived, a Wellington aircraft of this O.T.U, pranged into the nearby town, killing all the crew and a number of local inhabitants. The poignant point to me was that the wireless operator on board this aircraft, was an old friend of mine, way back in the ACRC and ITW days. How he had reached this stage of training ahead of me, I do not recall. Come to think of it though, I was hospitalised after my ITW course, thereby delaying my onward progression through the various training stages; how lucky can one get!

O.T.U, as all aircrew know, was for crewing up into a permanent bomber crew. Our Skipper was the only Officer amongst us, the rest of us being sergeants. The flying programme consisted of circuits and bumps, cross country navigational exercises, both day and night, and sundry other exercises to try and mould us into a team, prior to entering the world of operations. Lectures and other ground subjects were still very much a part of our education. A very necessary item was dinghy drill, which, if one could swim, was quite entertaining. One thing though that filled me with horror was the pressure chamber test. We all had to have a go in this 'thing'. To my relief however, I was not one of the guinea pigs selected to show the rest of us how oxygen starvation could affect one. It was partly due to this machine, and wearing my helmet and oxygen mask whilst flying, that I contracted Impetigo twice whilst at this O.T.U. I was not very popular with my crew as my incapacitation disrupted our training schedule. The disease, being a contagious one, resulted, much to my chagrin, in being locked away in the camps hospital isolation ward. I was not amused.

Whether it was due to this, or some other factor, our crew was posted to another O.T.U at Moreton in the Marsh. The thing that stands out in my mind about this place was that all the crews, with the exception of us, were Australians. These gentlemen, not noted for their blind obedience to service discipline, took exception to the dictatorial manner of our CO. He was an Englishman of the old school with old-fashioned ideas on service life. The Aussie aircrew very soon had the measure of this gentleman, thwarting his disciplinary measures. We, being the only English crew and delighted at this turn of events benefited accordingly.

I see from my logbook that our main pre-occupation at this station, was fighter affiliation. A change from cross-country exercises – corkscrewing around the skies, trying to avoid Spitfires and Hurricanes.

Our stay at this unit was short lived – about three weeks only – before being posted to the penultimate stage of our training, prior to joining a squadron, or so we thought.

This final training course was at No. 1668 HCU based at Cottesmore in Rutland, to be converted on to Lancaster's.

By this time the European war had finished and presumably the HCU attendance was in preparation for Tiger Force against the Japanese.

The Lanc: certainly from a Wireless Operator's position, was a beautiful aeroplane. For example, the back rest to one's seat in the radio compartment was the main spar of the aircraft. So, it was like sitting in an armchair, very comfortable, the best position of any crew member, even better than the pilots position! He was not enclosed, being surrounded by Perspex, although he did have an armour plated back rest. We Wireless Operators had another advantage in that we controlled the crews heating system, not always very popular with other crew members, as they either became too warm, or froze to death, whilst the likes of yours truly enjoyed a snug warmth.

Two more aircrew joined us at HCU to make up the normal Lanc: crew complement of seven, compared to only five of us in the Wellington.

Towards the end of this course, which we did complete, the Japanese conflict ended. At least I could claim that I had reached operational status but as there was no more fighting to be done, where do we go from here? Incidentally, I cannot deny that the majority of us heaved a big sigh of relief. From all accounts, the Japanese were not as kindly disposed towards POW's – if that would be our misfortune – as the Germans were. You could say our crew, and others had a lucky escape from both conflicts.

Now you will understand why I have described my R.A.F. career as a 'lovely' war. I had survived right through the training programme and, as a bonus, had not experienced a shot fired in anger. Being no hero, I had escaped the dangers of wartime very nicely. I did however experience some horrors of bombing and Flying Bombs (Doodle Bugs).

When on leave, I spent some of my time with my mother who lived throughout the war in London. Although I never experienced the blitz on London earlier of the early war years, occasionally during my visits to the capital, sporadic bombing did occur. One night in particular I remember very vividly. My mother's house was a three-storey building and, despite the air raid siren having been sounded, I elected to stay up top rather than descend into the basement, where there was a makeshift shelter. A huge explosion uncomfortably nearby rudely awakened my slumbers. That was enough for me. I shot out of bed and raced downstairs in record time! I learnt the next day that a landmine had exploded not two streets away.

As for flying bombs, I used to occasionally stay with my foster parents who lived near Guildford in Surrey. Their house was in that part of the green belt over which these pilotless missiles regularly flew, known as 'Doodle Bug Alley'. I saw a number of these machines flying close by, waiting for the dreaded silence when their engine stopped. Only one of these contraptions fell relatively close by, a mere couple of miles away. A bit near for comfort! This, if you can call it such, was my baptism of fire. Again I was fortunate to escape most of these unwelcome intrusions in wartime Britain.

Returning to my service life I discovered that I had not, after all, quite finished with flying. I was posted to No. 16 Ferry unit, of Transport Command, based at Dunkeswell in Devon.

This really was a sinecure of a job in that, all I did in six months at this unit was ferry Lancaster's to various MUs (Maintenance Units) around the countryside. Subsequently the object of this exercise was discovered. That wonderful aircraft were doomed for the scrap heap. A crying shame when one considers that of the over 7000 Lancaster's built, only one remains in flying shape, 50 plus years after they once crowded the night skies. Having already mentioned the esteem I felt for this machine and, although my involvement with them was minimal, I still count myself fortunate that I had flown in what many people consider was the greatest R.A.F. bomber of World War II. Even to this day, my interest in the Lanc has not diminished, as witness the personal library I have accumulated over the years concerning this particular aircraft.

Whilst at this Ferry Unit I only did three trips. The last one, to Valley on the Isle of Anglesey, was the most enjoyable one of all. The crew, being myself, the pilot and navigator (standard crew complement for ferry duties) were told there was no need to hurry back to base. We took this order literally – it took us a week to return to Dunkeswell. What we got up to, being three rather lively flyers, I will leave to the imagination of the readers. Nothing ventured; nothing gained!

I have deliberately refrained from expounding upon my flying activities, partly due to memory lapse but also, the indisputable fact that there are far more qualified persons of note, who have committed their flying experiences to print, as witness the number of books published on this subject.

My sole satisfaction, in relating my experiences, can be summed up by being judged fit by my peers, to operate solo in a bomber crew. I had overcome the 'screening' stage. I admit I would have welcomed, if that were the appropriate term to use, the chance to prove myself under fire.

On leaving the Ferry Unit, I joined the mass of redundant aircrew.

My first non-flying posting was to Pershore, which now had become a maintenance unit. For my three weeks tenure at this place I was given the delightful task of guarding the main gate. In other words I became a temporary SP (Service Policeman) a role I had NOT volunteered for. In fact, it was the last thing in the R.A.F. I wanted to do, having had the odd brush with these gentlemen in the past! To add insult to injury, most of my duties covered the dusk to dawn shift, which effectively ruined my social life. All night stuck in a guardroom did not appeal to my sense of humour. Thank God this position was short lived.

My final position was also to an MU, this time Bicester near Oxford. Initially, of all things, I found myself in the Station Warrant Officers office as his disciplinary NCO. My job was to draw up nightly guard duty rosters, relying to a large extent on 'volunteers'! Fortunately, for my sanity, it was 'discovered' that I was not really cut out for this type of employment. I could have told them that in first place! I was transferred to the Motor Transport (MT) section.

I had previously taught myself to drive an occupation I revelled in, although I never held a driving licence. The only restriction imposed was that I was confined to driving within the camp confines. I started off being a co-driver, accompanying a redundant Warrant Officer Pilot, on the 'Queen Mary' transporters, delivering aircraft bits and pieces to various other MUs around the country. Eventually I progressed to being the Camp Salvage Wagon driver – what a title! – driving a three tonner Bedford vehicle. For labouring I had half a dozen ex 'Africa Korps' boys, collared from a nearby POW camp. A more helpful bunch of men would have been hard to find. They flatly refused to let me do any manual work, I was purely their driver. It was hard to imagine they were once our enemies.

I remained in this job until I was demobbed. I finally left the R.A.F. at the demob: centre at Kirkham near Blackpool in Lancashire.

Little did I know it at the time but, many years later I would set up home not far from Kirkham, when I met my future wife Bette, whilst employed as a civilian flyer at Squires Gate aerodrome.

In conclusion, I look back on my four years in the R.A.F. as mainly a most enjoyable period in my life. Ironically enough, thanks to the war, I found my vocation in my subsequent chosen professions, firstly as a Radio Officer in civil aviation and secondly as an Air Traffic Control Officer.

How life can favour one's fortunes!

Before I recount my civil flying career there was one episode in my life that is perhaps worth a mention.

Not satisfied with having escaped one conflict I now proposed putting my head on the 'chopping block' for another! Although I had already started my civil flying career as a Radio Officer and, to boot, was gainfully employed as such, what happened next was as a direct result of the Korean War.

At the time I was living in London and, amongst my off-duty pleasure pursuits, was having the odd noggin at the renowned Brevet Club in Mayfair, of which I happened to be a member.

Unknown to me, a behind the scenes proposal between the American and British Governments had suggested the formation of a USAF B29 Bomber Squadron manned entirely by ex-RAF aircrew types, similar in concept to the wartime Eagle squadron of the American fighter pilots. Negotiations must have reached an advanced stage of implementation as, amongst other things, ranks, uniforms, pay scales etc, had already been agreed upon. We were told that we would be inducted into the USAF as Lieutenants, except the pilots, who would be Captains. The upshot of this high level proposal was that American Embassy in London, approached the Brevet Club asking for volunteers. Personally, being a naïve sort of person, the attraction of donning the uniform of a USAF 'Lootenant' with its attendant glamorous image, outweighed the possible dire consequences of what I could be letting myself in for.

As it happened, there were only three of us mad enough to offer our services: myself, an ex-pilot and a flight engineer. Hardly the basis for forming a squadron!

The possible public interest in this proposal was recognised by one of the principal London Evening papers, which sent along a reporter and photographer to record what they thought could be a historic event. Photographs were taken of us three stalwarts signing appropriate forms, in the Brevet Club, which duly appeared emblazoned on the front page of the accredited newspaper.

I can well remember being frightened to death as to what reaction my Mother would take if she saw her beloved son volunteering for such hazardous activities. As luck would have it, her regular London evening paper was NOT the one in which I appeared. I don't think she ever knew what I got up to!

Needless to say, due to the poor response, the Bomber Squadron never got airbourne. On reflection, pursuing peacetime employment, rather than entertaining war like activities was, yet again, a lucky escape from reality.

3 CIVVY STREET

Now that the R.A.F. had dispensed with my services, what career should I pursue? At this stage of my life I really had no idea what I wanted to do. I had a vague notion that I would like to go into the Automobile Industry. I liked cars and, in particular, driving them. Beyond that, I had little or no knowledge about them; the internal combustion engine was a mystery to me.

Mother, through her previously mentioned connections, tried to pull strings on my behalf, but to no avail. Maybe just as well, as I, in reality, didn't have much to offer in this field.

A chance meeting with an ex-R.A.F. Navigator colleague put me on the road to a career, which ultimately I was to pursue for the rest of my working life. He was studying for his civilian aircrew Navigator's licence and suggested I could do a lot worse than think on similar lines.

Thanks to Mother's encouragement and financial backing, I was enrolled in a London Technical Training College and, in due course, obtained the civilian Wireless Telegraphy Radio Operator's licence.

To try and obtain employment in civil aviation as a Radio Officer was another matter. As one can imagine, there were a lot of ex R.A.F. aircrew who had similar ideas to me. On obtaining their civilian licences, they too found that civil flying companies were swamped with job applications. Consequently, at this stage it was impossible to obtain employment; London, although the hub of civil aviation activity, had nothing to offer. As I was getting tired, not to mention the expense, of living in the Metropolis, I returned to my foster family who were by now living in Torquay. A delightful part of the U.K. and, if I had been of retirement age, I could have easily settled there for the rest of my natural life. A lot of water would flow under the bridge before I could consider such matters. I had all my adult life looming ahead but no immediate job prospects to look forward to. To try and remedy the situation, I even spent some time visiting all the aerodromes in the Southwest looking for vacancies. Pilot positions yes, but no openings for Radio Officers.

In the meantime, it became imperative that any employment should be considered.

The main Post Office in Torquay, it being roundabout Christmas time, was looking not only for part-time helpers to cope with the festive season, but also permanent staff. An ex-Navy friend of mine, and I, elected to join. I must admit that neither of us intended to spend the rest of our lives as Postmen. We enjoyed the perks of delivering Christmas parcels – tips and all that – but letter sorting into which we had been programmed, seemed a dead end way of earning a living. After three weeks of this caper, we had a test, in which we had to sort out so many letters into their respective pigeon holes, in a given time. We both failed this test miserably, by design. This was on a Friday. The following Monday, I went to the Labour Exchange and was amazed to find another job so quickly. I became a stores clerk with a local branch of the well-known carpet cleaner manufacturers Hoover. Many years later I reckon they were still trying to sort out my filing system, an administrative number that I had difficulty in coping with. By nature I think I was more the practical kind, rather than an office type but at least I was employed. All that studying I had done for my civilian flying ticket seemed to be getting me nowhere. In fact, I was getting so disillusioned that I sounded out the possibility of rejoining the R.A.F. in my old aircrew trade.

The Berlin Airlift – Airflight Ltd

One night, while I was still in Torquay, out of the blue I was offered a flying job. I received a phone call from the wife of the wartime Pathfinder Chief AVM D.C.T. Bennett asking whether I was interested in a Radio Officer's position in her husbands company. He was involved in the recently started Berlin Airlift. I didn't need a second asking. I accepted there and then. One week later I was in Germany. Where Mrs. Bennett got my name from I have no idea. Presumably there was an office somewhere in London that had a pool of licensed civilian aircrew personnel awaiting employment.

The circumstances as to how I got this job were a bit unusual. The Radio Officer I was replacing ha been involved in the well-known occasion when Bennett had taken off with his elevator locks in. This incident must have so unnerved the bloke I was replacing that, after the aircraft eventually landed, he was last seen disappearing out of the astrodome, so the story goes. His departure enabled me to embark on a career, which I have never looked back on since.

I travelled to Germany via the night ferry from Harwich to the Hook of Holland and thence by train to where I would start my civilian flying career, Wunstorf, a former Luftwaffe fighter aerodrome.

This was my first ever excursion away from the U.K. shores so, apart from anything else, it was very much a new experience in my life. The night ferry crossing was also the first time I had been to sea. Fortunately it was a smooth crossing, the sea being on its best behaviour. Not so the German train. It was most uncomfortable, with wooden seating making British trains positively luxurious by comparison.

Before arriving at Wunstorf I changed trains at Osnabruck which was a real eye opener to what damage Bomber Command had inflicted on a German City. I had never seen such devastation. Walking through the half-deserted streets was an eerie experience. Initially on arrival at Wunstorf I, like the rest of Bennett's aircrew, were billeted in the old German officers mess. Very plush accommodation, complete with all mod cons including a bowling alley in the basement! At a later date we were farmed out to the annexe, a collection of wooden huts, not quite so luxurious.

Airflight had two Tudor aircraft, being the long nosed version of this marque. In those days it was one of the largest aircraft in the world. Each aircraft carried nine tons of diesel oil in specially adapted fuel tanks fitted in the fuselage.

As there have been a number of books written about the Airlift, I will just mention the odd incident I experienced whilst engaged on this operation. On one occasion these tanks burst with the amount of oil being pumped in, leaving the inside of the aircraft in an unholy mess. Not hard to imagine the extent of the cleaning operation before the aircraft could be put back into service.

Occasionally whilst flying to Berlin on one of the aerial corridors that converged on that city, Russian fighters would 'buzz' us, no doubt to ensure we did not stray into their territory.

At the height of the operation, twenty-four hours a day, the density of aircraft was such that, if one missed one's approach into Berlin, you had to return to base and start all over again. There were three aerodromes in Berlin earmarked for this operation, namely Templehof, Tegel and Gatow. We flew into the last named.

I mentioned earlier the size of our aircraft. On one sortie we had to divert to an American base. They could not believe their eyes when they saw our machine. Even by their standards, it was enormous.

The British participation, in which I cut my teeth, was known as 'Plainfare'. To begin with, I was green as grass. I had a lot to learn about duties and responsibilities as a Radio Officer.

Bennett, being a notorious hard taskmaster, was a difficult man to please, therefore one had to work doubly hard to gain his confidence in one's performance. Not an easy task but, by degrees, as one built up experience, so one's efforts were gradually appreciated. You knew that time had come when he called you up by your Christian name. I had to wait some time for this accolade.

Being such a small comp any with the bare minimum of staff, a lot of the maintenance work was done by us aircrew. For example, we carted heavy radio equipment to and from the aircraft which, unfortunately, led to my following problem. I woke up one morning and noticed a lump protruding from my groin area. I thought oh no, I've done myself an injury. The station doctor confirmed my worst fears; I had ruptured myself. I was promptly returned to the U.K. for the necessary operation. This put me out of action for sometime. After a period of convalescence, I returned to Wunstorf to resume my flying duties.

I mention this if, for no other reason, as an indication that, despite my inexperience and hospitalisation, the AVM, as he was affectionately known by all and sundry, was willing to keep me on his payroll. He could quite easily have used my predicament to off-load me.

Not long after my return to Wunstorf, a tragic accident befell our other skipper Clem Utting, who I was flying with at the time, which resulted in his untimely death. On our flights to Gatow and, whilst awaiting the aircraft to be off-loaded its cargo, the crew repaired to the Malcom Club for refreshments. On this particular trip, we were walking back to the aircraft at about two in the morning. Clem was a few paces ahead of Stan Sicklemore (the First Officer) and myself when, without warning, a truck appeared from nowhere, knocking our skipper over, and sped off without stopping. Stan and I rushed over to the prone figure on the ground where it became painfully obvious that he was badly injured. He was barely conscious and thought he had crashed the aircraft. Whilst Stan and I sought help, the AVM at Wunstorf was contacted. Only he and Clem were authorised to fly the Tudor at night so, Stan and I were stuck in Gatow until our boss could cadge a lift and fly us back to base. Roundabout nine o'clock the same morning, Clem succumbed to his injuries.

At a later date, I attended the inquest into his death, in Berlin, but it was never discovered who was responsible.

Some years later, the well known author Richard Collier, wrote a book about the Airlift entitled 'Bridge Across The Sky' in which he refers to this incident and draws his own conclusions. He mentions me by name as one being involved in this unfortunate episode.

Another recollection I have is an occasion I have, flying back to Wunstorf; an engine failure necessitated dumping some of our fuel, in the middle of a thunderstorm. An operation, in itself of little consequence but getting rid of fuel in these circumstances didn't appear to be very safe. On reflection, I seem to remember we were surrounded by cunimbs at the time therefore, Our skipper presumably had no alternative but to do what he did.

On a lighter note, it was not a question of all work and no play. Because we were based in Germany part of our monthly salary was paid in BAFS (British Armed Forces of Occupation Currency) which, in our company, amounted to an allowance of approximately £14 per month and, it was dammed hard to spend that amount. For instance, one could get 'blotto' for less than five shillings. Cigarettes were about ten shillings for two hundred. Hanover, being the nearest town of note, you could stay in one of the remaining hotels left standing, for the princely sum of one shilling and sixpence covering evening meal, bed and breakfast: such extravagance. If one had coffee or chocolates to barter with the locals, the sky was the limit as to what one might receive in return!

On completion of the airlift I had done 155 lifts. If I hadn't ruptured myself half way through the operation, I might have almost doubled that figure. Looking back I was grateful to 'Pathfinder' Bennett employing me, subsequently to enjoy a successful and rewarding career.

Many years later I attended a re-union of Berlin Airlift aircrew, held at the RAF Museum Hendon. On arrival, I was greeted by a commissionaire with the words 'are you a veteran of the Airlift'. I never thought I would be addressed in such terms; it made me, feel a trifle ancient!

After the airlift, our Tudors, having been re-configured into passenger carrying aircraft, I found myself even further afield – India. My first taste of a really hot climate. The contract we had was taking freight to Karachi and then, on the return journey, bring Pakistan Air Force personnel to the U.K. This, for me, was a one-off trip. Little did I realise that, at a later date, I would return to India, transporting similar personnel from West Pakistan to East Pakistan, the later destination being Chittagong. En-route we re-fuelled in Delhi, which meant our 'troops', had to travel in mufti to avoid complications with the Indian authorities. These were the days of partition between India and Pakistan. Come to think of it, isn't that still the case?

On a different theme, an indication of the AVM's well known attitude towards petty officialdom is, I think, worth recording. Not for anything did he enjoy the soubriquet 'The stormy petrel of civil aviation'.

To set the scene, what I am about to relate, happened on a flight to Rome. On the way we made a re-fuelling stop at Geneva.

When ready for departure, for some reason or other, air traffic Control refused us take-off clearance. What happened next could be likened to an episode from the 'Keystone Cops', of the silent movies era. ATC at Geneva had instructed the airport ground staff to wheel chock our aircraft until, whatever the problem was, could be resolved. Bennett, frustrated at this delay in our departure, instructed his first officer (the imperturbable Stan Sicklemore) to exit the aircraft by the rear door and remove the chocks. As soon as he had done this and re-entered the aircraft, the ground staff promptly replaced the chocks. This scenario was enacted two or three times before Bennett, in exasperation, opened up the engines to get the aircraft moving at a pace too fast for the chock boys to continue playing their little game. Eventually, we took-off without ATC clearance. What the Swiss authorities thought about this apparent flouncing of their rules and regulations, s not recorded. Maybe the fact that Bennett was married to a Swiss Lady smoothed the ruffled feathers of officialdom.

On this same flight the aircraft's eventual destination was Johannesburg. I was to be off-loaded at Lydda in Palestine, to take part in another operation. Due to what happened next, I was very glad indeed that I was not to continue this flight. On approaching Lydda there crept into the cockpit a most unpleasant and nauseating smell. There were no visible signs, such as fire or smoke, to cause such a stench. What had happened was that the aircraft batteries had boiled over? If anyone has experienced such a problem, they will know exactly how I felt. I sympathised with the crew who had to continue on this flight. Incidentally, I have often wondered if what I had experienced, had anything to do with the two Tudors that disappeared on the South American run. How a crew could continue operating under such circumstances beggars belief. Pure conjecture I know.

The operation I next became involved in was a form of mini airlift. Our task was to transport Yemenites from Aden to Palestine, or was it Israel – I forget – to the promised land, as they called it. For the duration of this charter, we were alternatively based in Aden and Lydda. I thought India was hot but Aden took the biscuit. The heat was almost unbearable. The only saving grace being that, when we night-stopped their, our hotel was air-conditioned. When not flying we had the use of a nearby beach, cordoned off from marauding sharks, to cool off in; not that the sea was much cooler than the land!

The Yemenites were a very primitive race. We transported a hundred plus of these individuals at a time and, such was their poor physical condition, coupled with their distinct lack of hygiene (the stench of these people was awful) that on arrival at Lydda, some of these hapless people did not survive the flight; they had died during transit.

To look after 'our' passengers were couriers especially trained to cope with their charges unusual needs? For example, on one classic occasion, some of our passengers decided that a fire, on board the aircraft, would be a good idea to do there cooking by. Fortunately, the couriers were quick off the mark, and smartly nipped this idea in the bud. We didn't learn about this until after we had landed, as our crew compartment was sealed off from the passenger cabin. The mind boggles as to what might have happened!

Changing the subject for a moment, one might ask what were the duties of a Radio officer in these, and other similar regions. As I have indicated before, Air Traffic Control, as we now know it, was then in its infancy and, therefore, out job was to establish and maintain communication between ourselves and the ground agencies that monitored our flights, giving the following information in relation to the progress of one's flight e.g. our position, height, speed etc. at regular intervals. All this was conducted in Morse code by wireless telegraphy, key bashing in other words. In addition, listening to and recording weather broadcasts. Our duties, as outlined, were of particular importance when flying over sparsely populated and remote areas, such as we were doing on this route and other similar routes later on in my flying career. Only in the vicinity of airports did R/T (radio telephony) communication gradually supersede wireless telegraphy. For the present though, Radio Officer's were an important part of an airliner's crew complement.

My next flight was, by contrast, an endurance test of my stamina. For starters, the AVM was one of those remarkable men whose physical make-up, quite apart from his other attributes, enabled him to operate with minimal rest periods. At the material time, his company was still engaged in the transport of Pakistani servicemen across India. I was to go out there, once the Yemenite lift had been completed.

What I was not prepared for was a flight, in a twin engined low airspeed light aircraft (an Airspeed Consul) flown by Bennett with me as his Radio Officer. We departed Blackbushe one early morning and ended up in Karachi 48 hours later, with so-called night-stop on route, in Rome – all four hours of it! The AVM was as fresh as a daisy as we touched down at Karachi. I, on the other hand, needed matchsticks to keep my eyes open! I don't think I was much use to him anyway on this flight, as the radio equipment, on this aircraft, was foreign to me. Not that he needed my services as, being the master navigator he was, he planned and executed the whole flight, literally on the back of a postcard.

My time with Airflight covered just over twelve months during which I accumulated my first civilian 723 flying hours.

Although, much as I admired and respected Bennett, the only reason I left his employ was solely due to the hectic flying schedules we were expected to maintain. In other words let's be frank, I was looking for a less strenuous flying number. Ironically, whilst serving my notice, I was sharing a flat with the R/O who perished in the LLANDOW accident. The tragic occasion when one of our Tudor's, carrying Rugby football supporters crashed on landing, killing all on board. The skipper had been my regular pilot and the last man I had flown with before giving my notice.

William Dempster Ltd – April-July 1950

This company, oddly enough, was another Tudor operator who was engaged mainly in carrying passengers to and from Johannesburg.

The Tudor, despite its unfortunate disappearing 'act' reputation which I have already referred to was, in my opinion, a delight to fly in, albeit I only flew in the long nosed versions. The 'lost without trace' aircraft were the short nosed marques. I count myself lucky to have flown over 700 hours in them, without incident. On these trips to Johannesburg I saw quite a lot of Africa, albeit mainly from the air. Most of the airports we called at were of a reasonable standard. The odd one though, was just a landing strip hacked out of the bush, with a very rudimentary terminal complex.

Whilst with this company, by way of a change, I was seconded to their parent South African outfit, Pan African air Charter, and flew in their South African registered aircraft, a Dakota. On one occasion we carried two dismantled helicopters; an unusual cargo. The other trips I did in this aircraft were passenger charters. Another out of the ordinary kind of flying was conducted in a DH Dove, where I sat alongside the pilot. A nice change from being tucked away in a crew compartment divorced from the sharp end of the aircraft. In this machine we did a couple of trips to a delightful seaside town on the eastern shores of South Africa, called Margate.

Admittedly my stay with this company was short lived but, at least, I was broadening my horizon, and adding more flying time.

Crewsair Ltd – August 1950-September 1951

For a change in scene and aircraft, I found myself based at Southend flying at first in Dakota's; later this company up-dated its fleet to the more modern and faster Vickers Viking.

Our main work was charter flights carrying passengers to destinations predominantly in the European and Mediterranean area, interspersed with the odd African flight, to make life that more interesting.

I cannot recall anything untoward happening during my time with this company but, a list below, will give some indication of the varied nature of our charter flight places that we visited which included Nice, Malta, El Adem, BASLE, Lydda, Lyons, Schipol, Rome, Tarbes, Paris,

Marseille, Oslo, Zurich, Lille, Buckeburg, Nicosia, Pisa, Malpensa, Stockholm, Copenhagen, Reims, and Helsinki. Though not necessarily in that order. In fact, you name it, we were almost certain to have been there. As for the African flights, we traversed the length and breadth of the African continent. For example, our itinerary included the following ports of call: – Khartoum, Juba, Entebbe, Tabora, Lusaka, Johannesburg, Kumalo, Wadi Halfa, Kasama, Bulawayo, Malakal, Kisumu, Nakuru, Ndola, Mtubatuba, a real jungle cleared airstrip, Dar-es-Salaam, Salisbury, Wadi Seidna, Luxor, etc. I think similar comments could apply to this list, as indicated on the previous one.

Still with the same company and, not to be outdone, we occasionally went as far afield as Karachi via Baghdad, Sharjah, Basra, Jiwani and all points in between, from our base at Southend.

People used to say to me "aren't you lucky visiting all these exotic places, and getting paid for it". Very true, but of all the countries and places we went to, in reality, all we saw were airports and, on night stops, the hotel, nearby bars and nightclubs. Not that I complained mind you! Opportunities to explore different country localities were rare. However, on some of the African flights, we did manage the odd game reserve visit.

Up to this point in the flying game, apart from our airborne responsibilities, we did most of our own ground handling as well. Nowadays, this latter part of the aviation scene is catered for by appointed ground-handling agents.

During my flying duties with this company I did experience one rather unusual occurrence.

I was flying in a Dakota from somewhere in southern France back to our base at Southend. On approaching the Paris area we became confronted with an enormous Cunimb, thunderstorm to the uninitiated, which seemed to stretch to infinity either side of us and above, blocking our intended flight path.

Now, as anyone in the flying game knows, aircrew and their passengers are not supposed to fly above 10,000 feet without either oxygen or the benefit of being enclosed in a pressurised cabin. The Dakota, for all its attributes, had neither facility.

Nothing daunted, our skipper decided there was no alternative but to try and fly over the top of the storm, bearing in mind that such weather phenomena can reach enormous heights. The Dak: managed to stagger up to just over 18,000 feet by, which time, I had succumbed to the rarified air. To put it bluntly, I became incapable of carrying out my normal wireless operating function. I found myself prone on the floor of the aircraft, beside the radio compartment.

What astonished me was that our skipper, being slight of build and stature, didn't seem to be one bit affected and, I suspected, wondered what all the fuss was about when he saw me inert on the floor.

Needless to say, somehow we overcame the elements and eventually landed back at base without further ado. An occurrence I only experienced once in my flying career.

Talking of thunderstorms, there would be many occasions during my flying career where we had to contend with these horrors of nature. Most times one could avoid them, but occasionally there would be no alternative but to plough through these storms.

This meteorological phenomenon invariably contains icing conditions and hail within it. Consequently the battering an aircraft took, what with ice being flung off the propeller blades, hailstones hitting the fuselage, the noise, the extremes of turbulence, could all be a bit unnerving. On one occasion I had forgotten to reel in my trailing aerial. The next thing there was a blinding flash and my aerial had disappeared!

Hunting Air Travel – September 1951-August 1952

For my next flying appointment I was based at Bovingdon in Hertfordshire. Before anyone gets the wrong impression, the reason I switched flying jobs so regularly was solely to improve my financial status, not to mention the fact that 'variety is the spice of life'. Despite my apparent restlessness, I never suffered the ignominy of dismissal.

Huntings were exclusively a Viking aircraft company. A lot of our work was flying service personnel and their families to Malta and, to a lesser extent, Gibraltar. A bit mundane after the variety of charter flights in which I had been involved in my previous companies. On the plus side, this company was better organised than previous ones. In particular the ground handling was dealt with by specialized ground staff. We were now strictly aircraft crew members. All other aspects were taken care of, by other agencies.

I see from my log book that we did, at one time, have a regular run to Lagos and even the odd trip to Nairobi.

One of the highlights of the Lagos trips was that after we had disembarked the aircraft and deposited our night stop gear in the hotel, we were transported to a nearby beach restaurant where a long table was laid out with just about every kind of culinary delight imaginable. If, like me, you were a curry addict, they were one of the best I had ever come across, complete with all the side dishes that a good curry warrants. To complete the meal, there was ice-cold beer with which to wash it down! After that, a bit of swimming and sunbathing constituted the climax of a perfect day. Pity we didn't do these trips more often.

The only time I flew in another type of aircraft, whilst with this firm, was a couple of short flights in a Dakota.

We did a stint, at one time, on behalf of British European Airways (BEA) operating their Northolt/Dublin schedules. A taste of how a national carrier performs.

Due to the predominance of our Malta flights, regular night stops became common and Hunting's acquired their own accommodation on the island. It was a sort of guesthouse staffed by the locals to attend to our needs.

Malta, I confess, was not one of my favourite places at which to spend any time. As far as I was concerned, all it was fit for was eating, drinking and sleeping. There were few decent beaches around for swimming and sunbathing, albeit the climate was conducive to such leisurely pastimes. As for entertainment, the notorious 'GUT' was about the only place for amusement. Anyone who has been to Malta will have heard, if not visited, this place. It was a street in the capital Valetta full of dubious nightclubs. Some of the female 'artistes' were old enough to be one's grandmother! If nothing else, it was good for a laugh.

Whilst on the subject of accommodation, and leaving the flying side of my activities for a moment, a brief look of how I spent my life, between flying duties, is possibly illuminating, to say the least!

I, and two colleagues, all being R/O's based at Bovingdon and, to boot, unattached from a domestic point of view, decided to share 'digs' in Berkhamsted, the nearest town to Bovingdon aerodrome. This arrangement worked quite well until our various landlords and landladies took exception to our life-style, and some of the antics we got up to. So, pastures new had to be sought.

It so happened that our local 'watering' hole, the Swan in Berkhamsted high street where admittedly we spent most of our off duty time, had some rooms to let. So, without further ado, we moved in lock, stock and barrel. The trouble with this arrangement was the landlord! He was also a horse racing correspondent whose idea of a night out, was to invite us renegades to accompany him in the 'snug' bar, after closing time, for all night drinking and card gambling sessions. We enjoyed our newfound life-style for five years. There were times though, where this constant imbibing got the better of us and, by way of a change, once a week we visited the local cinema, no matter what films were being shown. Having said that, one should never look a gift horse (how appropriate!) in the mouth!

Back to reality and my next job. Literally I crossed one of the taxiways at Bovingdon to join the other resident company operating at this aerodrome.

Lancashire Aircraft Corporation – Sept-Nov 1952

You will note, from the time I spent with this company, that it was a short stay but, as it happened, I was to re-join them at a later date.

I was now flying in the Avro York, the civilian version of the famous WWII Lancaster bomber. The few trips I did were trooping flights to Fayid in the Egyptian Canal Zone.

Later on this company moved their base to Stansted in Essex.

My short stay was due to an opportunity to further my career. An opportunity which I would have been a fool to ignore.

The Swiss National Airline Swissair was advertising for R/O's. My present employer was prepared to release me, if I was successful in my application. Not only that, but if at a later date I wished to return to them, they would be happy to re-employ me subject to there being a vacancy. With that kind of attitude I couldn't lose.

Swissair – January-August 1953

Myself and an ex BEA R/O were accepted and made our home in Zurich, Swissair's main base of operations. The first real scheduled Airline I had ever become involved in. The aircraft I would fly in were Convairs and DC4's which covered most of Swissair's European route structure.

After a period of training, we qualified as Bordfunkers; what a title to be landed with, sounds positively disgusting doesn't it! This name is in fact a literal German translation of a Radio Officer. The licence they issued was in fact a Radio/Navigators licence, although we never touched navigation.

On these European routes it so happened that we Bordfunkers rarely, if ever, touched a Morse key. All our destinations were within Radio-Telephony range. Consequently our main responsibility was to record all R/T transmissions, both air to ground and vice versa and note down Wireless Telegraphy weather broadcasts applicable to whatever route we were flying. In addition, we were responsible for logging scheduled time keeping, an all-important part of Swissair's operations. Questions were asked whenever flights were late or delayed.

The Convair was a delightful aircraft to fly in and, as most Swissair pilots were part-time military fighter pilots, some of them tended to pilot their Convairs in a similar manner. It didn't seem to bother the passengers.

One pilot in particular that I had the pleasure of flying with occasionally was an ex R.A.F. Bomber pilot by the name of Perry Wagner. He held dual nationality status. There was also an English DC4 co-pilot with whom I sometimes flew. They were like a breath of fresh air compared with some of the pure Swiss fellows I flew with. As the latter gentlemen originated from the German speaking part of Switzerland, their outlook on life was not dissimilar to their Teutonic neighbours. They were rather dour and lacking in the sense of humour stakes! Nevertheless they were highly efficient professionals. Maybe I'm being over critical but their up-bringing and general life style appeared to me to be lacking the free and easy way of an Englishman's way of life. By contrast, those Swiss who originated from the French speaking part of their country, around the Geneva area, seemed to be more attuned to our way of life. There was no doubt that Swissair, in all departments, were highly efficient in the conduct of their operations. I once had a look round one of their hangars and was struck by the cleanliness of the hangar floor. It was spotless – one could have eaten off them!

Returning to the flying side of things, although most of the flights I was involved in were of a routine nature, occasionally a number came up which is best described as a prolonged pleasure flight. Using the Convair, we did trips from Zurich to Geneva, weaving in and out of the mountaintops. This type of flying could be a bit hairy, as anyone who has flown amongst mountainous terrain will bear witness. The up and down draughts generated in these regions, could be a trifle unnerving. Nevertheless, the scenery was spectacular to say the least. Naturally, from a safety angle, these flights were only conducted under favourable weather conditions.

To sum up then, flying with a world renowned and highly efficient airline, was an experience not to be missed. In the eight months I spent with them, I added a further 403 flying hours to my overall total, not to mention the invaluable experience of flying with an International Carrier.

I won't go into the reasons why I left their employ but, suffice to say, it was NOT through any lack of expertise as a Bordfunker. I was never able to get used to this 'job description' I was labeled with!

Swissair must have been reasonably pleased with my performance as, despite the parting of our ways, they gave me a fair reference.

Skyways – September 1953-December 1956

I was not sorry to return home having lived in a foreign country with a different mode of living and culture, not to mention having to cope with language problems. I admit I am basically a home bird and, as far as learning to speak another language, I am a typical Englishman abroad who expects everyone to speak English; a negative attitude I know.

My previous employer, the Lancashire Aircraft Company were as good as their word and re-employed me. I carried on as though I hadn't left in the first place.

There were two changes to the company I was re-joining, namely their title had been changed to Skyways, and their permanent base was Stansted, instead of Bovingdon. So, it was back to the good old, if noisy, York aircraft. Their Rolls Royce Merlin engines created quite a din. In fact, after seven hours in one of these machines, a regular elapsed time on our Stansted/Malta run, my ears used to 'sing' for hours afterwards. Other aircrew experienced the same thing.

I did a few Fayid, via Malta, trips carrying service personnel to and from the Egyptian Canal Zone.

Due to the political situation that existed between Egypt and Palestine (or was it Israel, I forget!), these trooping flights on the first leg of the journey i.e. Stansted to Malta, were operated as a civil charter, crewed by civilian aircrew. Now comes the interesting part of these charters. The second half of these flights i.e. Malta to Fayid, was conducted, to all intents and purposes, as military flights.

To complete the illusion politically, our aircraft were adorned with both civilian and military markings though without, in the latter case, R.A.F. roundels. Likewise, us aircrew became instant R.A.F. aircrew officers complete with Identity cards and uniforms. Our skippers were Flight Lieutenants, the rest of us Flying Officers except the cabin crew, who were senior NCOs. For tropical uniforms we were given a monetary allowance to purchase our own. For my sins, I blew the lot on a celebratory booze-up! Consequently my tropical outfit had to come from my own pocket! The only trouble with this set-up was that one needed a larger than normal suitcase to house two uniforms, and civilian clothes for use when night stopping in Malta.

One memorable flight sticks out in mind. It occurred on a night flight from Fayid to Malta. The skipper, with whom I regularly flew, invited me once we were airborne to try my hand at manually flying the aircraft. As I hadn't much to do apart from routine position reports and obtaining weather reports for our destination aerodrome, I accepted his offer and ended up by practically flying the aircraft all the way to Malta, managing to keep on course and maintain height despite some rather nasty weather en route. I had done some 'stick pushing' previously and although having never aspired to be a pilot, I enjoyed the experience. The skipper must have had faith in my abilities as he 'slept' most of the way; the passengers were none the wiser!

At a later date an equally interesting number came up. I found myself based in Cyprus for a couple of months, trooping again, from Nicosia to Fayid. Further opportunities arose for hands on flying arose which made a welcome change to key bashing.

At this juncture I would like to record a peculiar trait that I discovered among some of the pilots with whom I flew. In my opinion, and I don't think I was alone in my observations, the most competent four engined 'drivers of airframe' were ex wartime fighter pilots. Men like 'Pancho Villa' who was one of the 'few' in the Battle of Britain, complete with DFC and bar. Others who come to mind were Tony Zeigberg, Rex Mulliner and Bob Hornall, to name a few.

All in all the aircrew in this company were a great bunch of characters. My boss, the Chief Radio Officer, Jock Hamilton, appeared to have had a charmed life. He was involved in three serious prangs in which, on each occasion, he was the sole survivor and, despite his traumatic experiences, continued to fly. He too was a holder of the DFC. Whilst on a similar theme, during the whole of my flying career, I can only recall one occasion when I felt ill in the air. That, as it turned out, was my own fault.

One of our infrequent night stops was Khartoum, when I was flying with a previous company; a place almost as hot as Aden if that is possible. Giant fans suspended from the ceiling cooled all the beds in our overnight hotel accommodation. Here was the catch though. If you chose to sleep on top of the bed sheet instead of underneath it, immediately below the whirring fan, the next day would invariably tell you that it was unwise to sleep in the tropics without some covering over your body. Sure enough, as I continued my journey on the morrow, I became an inanimate object lying in the back of the aircraft, distinctly feeling the worse for wear, unable to perform my duties as a Radio Officer. It taught me a valuable lesson of how to cope with sleeping in hot climates; a trap I never fell into again.

Whilst on the subject of aircrew sickness it was an inescapable fact of life that those few of us who did not partake of the waters, the alcoholic kind, tended to suffer all sorts of stomach upsets, particularly when transiting hot climates.

Not that I am implying that the majority of us were hardened drinkers, but a little bit of the hard stuff did wonders in keeping us fit, despite temperature changes and sampling oriental cuisine. I am happy to say I belonged to the latter breed of aviators.

Having got those items off my chest, albeit I think such comments are worth recording, I will return to the present, narrative wise.

Cyprus, compared with Malta, was a delightful island. It was a bonus to be based there with an equitable climate, sandy beaches and plenty of places to wine, dine and enjoy local hospitality and entertainment. This was; of course, the days before the troubles beset this lovely island.

I see from my logbook that I flew with the same skipper whilst based in Cyprus. His name was Reg Stokes, a big man with an enormous beard. He looked more like a naval type rather than an ex R.A.F. man. He too, quite often, let me loose with the controls as the trips were comparatively short and consequently not much wireless operating to do.

Upon returning home, after the completion of this middle east contract, another nice little number came my way.

As it happened, I was the only Radio Officer in the company who had comparative recent experience on Dakota's radio gear. Because of this fact, I was seconded to the parent company, Lancashire Aircraft Corporation, based at Blackpool, to carry out a VIP charter around Europe transporting two American Generals and their wives. My pilot was Jonnie Johnson, Blackpool's Chief Pilot and a gentleman with whom I was to have quite a number of dealings in the future years, pleasurable ones I might add! This trip lasted six days and, amongst our night stops was Kristiansand, Oslo, Copenhagen, Malmo, and Le Bourget. Not exactly a hectic schedule, the longest leg being of four hours duration and the shortest being all of twenty minutes, that being Copenhagen to Malmo, after which we again night stopped due fatigue!

An interesting episode whereby I could truly claim to have earned my spurs occurred on the Manchester to Kristiansand leg of our European journey. The weather at Kristiansand was such that the only way we could find the airport was by means of Direction Finding (D/F) bearings obtained by yours truly. This was one of the few occasions where my services, even if I say it myself, resulted in a successful landing, under very adverse weather conditions. Remembering my lack of recent experience on this particular aircraft's radio equipment I was particularly pleased. In fact, I recall the skipper and his co-pilot commenting on the fact that, without my input, they doubted that a successful landing could have been achieved.

This secondment to Blackpool whetted my appetite to the extent that I persuaded the powers to be that a permanency in this neck of the woods would be most welcome. My request was granted and before I knew what was happening, I was crewed up with Alec Watson (a former BEA pilot) and dispatched to Hamburg, on a semi permanent basis. The flights we did there were all passenger charters around the European theatre with the occasional foray to the U.K.

As it turned out I was to spend a further eighteen months based at Hamburg. What better place to be based, with all the delights this city had to offer, not forgetting the renowned Reeperbahn. Initially I was still a single person. However that status would alter due circumstances that for which I would always be thankful. In being detached to Blackpool I met my future wife Bette on one of my breaks from flying duties. You could say that Blackpool was to prove a most fortunate choice of venue on two accounts. Namely finding someone who was prepared to share my life and, on the second account, provide me with a place of work for the rest of my career, both flying and later in Air Traffic Control.

After our honeymoon I took my bride to our first home, a rented flat near the main railway station of Hamburg. Some would say this was like 'taking coals to Newcastle'! As far as I was concerned, nothing was further from the truth. I had got fed up with being a roaming minstrel and, despite the obvious attractions Hamburg had to offer, I was more than happy to have my wife with me. She took a hell of a gamble in marrying me as we had only known each other, on and off, for five months. In fact, on the day we got married it was only the 24th time we had met. She is a Yorkshire lass with true grit that is the hallmark of those particular county folk.

A never to be forgotten milestone in my life and, as I write this, here we are forty-two years later, still together.

Apart from all the Dakota trips I did, we also had Yorks, in which I did quite a number of night mail runs to Berlin Templehof, the pre-war Lufthansa Berlin base, was now the airport we flew into. Its construction was odd in that, in one take off direction one took-off or landed between blocks of flats, in between which there was a cemetery. The other direction was semi blocked by an elevated underground (U-Bahn) station. The point I am trying to make is that there wasn't much room for error in the event of an engine failure or some other hazardous occurrence.

On the odd trip I took Bette with me where we stayed in the American Officers Mess, for the princely sum of one shilling and sixpence, bed and breakfast. On one night out in Berlin, I nearly lost Bette in the Russian Zone, after a lover's tiff in a nearby nightclub. Berlin was a divided city and, if one inadvertently strayed into the Russian Zone, you were not welcome. We were lucky.

During the summer months we did the occasional charter to Palma in Majorca. On one of these trips I took my better half with me. We flew to Palma and returned, via Stockholm, leaving there at seven in the morning and arriving back in Hamburg at half past ten at night. One of the longest days I had ever spent in the flying game.

I had now become the chief R/O in our Hamburg based company, there being only two of us anyway, not a lot of satisfaction in that sort of promotion!

On a more sombre note, Hamburg was the scene of one of three lucky escapes I had throughout my flying career. On this occasion one of our Yorks had crashed in the Russian Zone en-route to Berlin. If I had not been in the U.K. on a short visit to see my fiancée, I could well have been aboard this aircraft. My two previous escapes from disaster, where I had drawn the lucky straw, were firstly when I was with Huntings and I switched aircraft at the last moment. The aircraft I should have been on crashed into Sicilian mountains. Prior to that was the Llandow prang, which I have already mentioned. I can only conclude that I had led a charmed life, not dissimilar to the 'cats and their nine lives' syndrome. Someone upstairs was obviously watching over me, despite the fact that I am agnostic as far as religion goes.

Whilst in Hamburg I got involved in, reputedly, the first German charter company to be formed post war. Lufthansa, their national carrier, had already started up again, partly crewed by British aircrew initially. Our aircraft was a German registered Dakota, with an English skipper, Audrey Vernon, a real smoothie but a nice guy, who once chased after my wife at a Christmas party held at Hamburg Airport! To complete the crew we had a German first officer and hostess, and myself. Was I involved in a little bit of history making?

Eventually all good things come to an end. Due my flying commitments being somewhat curtailed during the latter part of my stay in Hamburg, Bette and I could look upon this early period in our married life, as an extended honeymoon. Our first born, he eventually became an Airline pilot, was conceived whilst we were there. We returned to the U.K. in November 1955 and stayed with Bette's parents until we bought our own house, just up the road.

The following January, I was off on my travels yet again on what turned out to be an eventful and interesting change from the normal scheme of things. One of Blackpool's Dakotas, plus two others from Morton Air Services (Croydon) were chartered to accompany the 1965 Royal Tour of Nigeria. Our role on this trip was to carry the Queen's wardrobe, and members of the Press and TV media.

My skipper, Eric Skemp, was someone I had flown with before. A man I had a lot of time for; a born pilot. We duly set off from Blackpool and, amongst the places we stopped over en-route to Lagos, our base for the duration of the Royal Tour, were Gibraltar, Casablanca, Cape Juby, Villa Cisneros (a Spanish outpost and a very basic aerodrome) Port Etienne, Bathurst, Freetown, Robertsfield and Abidjan.

We spent almost three weeks in Lagos. Not a lot of flying was done whilst we were there so we took advantage of Lagos's premier social and swimming club, spending our time swimming, sun-bathing and generally lazing about.

On the occasions we were required to follow the Royal Couple about, we called at Kaduna, Jos, Enugu, Part Harcourt, Benin, and Ibadan. A Viking of the Queens Flight was used for flying the Queen and Duke about and, on one memorable occasion, we attended a tribal Durbah at Kano, in company with our royal charges.

Before our return to the UK I developed a head cold, which I could not shake off, not helped by the humidity of Lagos, which must have been 70-80%.

Because of my cold, we couldn't fly higher than 2000 feet. Our return journey was delayed even further by spending three days in Dakar to try and remedy my sickness. Still I couldn't shake it off much to my crews chagrin. We had to continue our journey homewards at the same height as before. Bearing in mind that we were traversing Europe in the middle of winter, our enforced low altitude flight path, which amongst other factors embraced the notoriously turbulent Bay of Biscay, was not a recommended practice under normal circumstances. I was not very popular!

Not content with subjecting my colleagues to this unorthodox kind of flying, we were carrying crates of gifts given to the Royal couple on their tour, destined for Buckingham Palace. They arrived rather late!

This trip ended my secondment to Blackpool. Now I was faced with commuting back and forth to Stansted, a lengthy drive particularly as it was before the Motorway system came into being. As I said earlier I had bought a house near the airport not far from my in-laws. The house purchase proved to be a good move as being faced with being away from home for lengthy periods at least my wife had her parents close to home to help when our first born arrived on the scene.

My next flight compared to what lay ahead were shortish ones, mainly to Malta and Cyprus. Re: the latter venue, a disturbing event occurred at Nicosia our destination airport in Cyprus. One of the companies later acquisitions a HP Hermes was blown up by EOKA terrorists, fortunately whilst the aircraft was still on the tarmac at

Nicosia. These were the days when terrorism beset Cyprus. I wasn't on this aircraft I flew down the following day in a York and saw the remains of this machine. Apart from the wings outboard the outer engines, it was an unrecognisable mess. It was a; lucky escape for the passengers and crew due solely to the skipper deciding that he had too much fuel on board. During the offloading period, the explosive device went off. Incidentally, as we were carrying service personnel and their families, maybe that was the reason we were targeted. Subsequent investigation revealed that a bottle of squash, with an explosive and timing device fitted, had gone off in the galley department which, on this type of aircraft was situated between the cockpit and the passenger compartment. It doesn't bear thinking about if the skipper hadn't noticed that he was overloaded with fuel.

Ultimately I was destined to spend most of the remainder of my flying days on the Singapore run. Again, a trooping contract and, to me, my first introduction to the Hermes aircraft. From my point of view it was undoubtedly the most spacious and comfortable civilian aircraft I have ever flown in. Apart from being away from home for lengthy periods I enjoyed these trips. On average the Singapore run, there and back, took three weeks, what with night stops and slipping crews on route. To think nowadays, such journeys can be done in one hop of 12 hours or less.

Perhaps of interest, our regular route was Stansted, Brindisi, Beirut, Bahrain, Karachi, Delhi, Calcutta, Bangkok and Singapore. Apart form the night stops on route Singapore was a must. In the latter case, one thing always stood out in my mind, which I can only put down to having a rather vivid imagination. On landing at Singapore, after which we were bussed from the airport to our hotel, we used to pass the infamous Changi jail. I couldn't but help thinking, when passing this place, what horrors must have been perpetrated by the Japanese in this notorious establishment.

Calcutta was another night stop of note. The crew bus ride from Dum-Dum airport to our hotel in the centre of Calcutta was through places of utter squalor and degradation. What the resident population had to put up with almost defied description. How lucky I used to think that, by comparison, we lived in a civilised country.

Before I packed up the flying game, by way of a change and, incidentally, one of my last flights, was a trip in a York to Keflavik (Iceland), the furthest west I have ever flown. We were carting a couple of spare engines for Pan American Airlines. What struck me were the short day light hours in this part of the world. No sooner had we arrived in daylight than night descended upon us.

Do I have any regrets during my flying career? Only that I never got as far as North America and Canada. Other places or countries, with the exception of Hong Kong I was not bothered about. The latter place, above all else, I would love to have seen.

In some ways I look upon my involvement in civil flying as being connected with the semi pioneering days of post war civil aviation. That fact alone was, to me, an interesting era to be involved in. I enjoyed the variety of places visited, the different aircraft types flown, above all, the camaraderie of the crews I flew with. They, being mostly ex war time R.A.F. types of similar age, and outlook, to myself.

For my money, I came into this sphere of aviation at the right time, and left before it became too technical and hide bound by rules and regulations.

Why was my flying days coming to a close? I could see the writing on the wall as to the future employment of R/O's. In the European and Mediterranean theatre of operations, radiotelephony (R/T) had virtually replaced the former wireless telegraphy (W/T) method of communication. Consequently airlines flying these routes, were dispensing with the services of R/O. Even on the longer and less populated barren routes the imminent advent of the Jet aircraft age, being much faster and higher flying machines compared to the propeller driven aircraft, the requirement for R/Os was becoming questionable. Skyways did offer me conversion to become a pilot, which was very tempting but due to my oncoming phobia mentioned below it was just as well I didn't go ahead with their generous offer. There was no denying the fact that I had survived an accident-prone era; maybe my nerves were getting the better of me!

Anyway, with these warning signs rearing their ugly heads I thought to myself, the sooner I transferred to a ground number, hopefully remaining within the aviation scene, the better my prospects with getting involved in an other aviation connected profession, would be.

Air Traffic Control appealed to me as an ideal alternative way of earning a living. I duly applied to the ATC hierarchy and was pleasantly surprised to be invited to attend an interview board. I must have created the right impression as I was duly taken on board. This was to be my professional role for the rest of my working life right up to the grand old age of 70, which I never regretted for one moment.

I had enjoyed a civilian-flying career for nine years, and amassed a grand total of 6250 hours. This, of course, was in the days before aircrew hours were restricted which, if I had been flying during the letter era of civil aviation, I doubt that I would have accrued the amount of flying time I had. Interestingly, a couple of aircraft I had flown in, I managed to do over a thousand hours in, they being Dakota and Viking. Even on the Tudor, I wasn't far short of the magical thousand. Maybe, as hinted to earlier, it was just as well I terminated my flying career when I did as, gradually I developed a phobia about flying; a variant of the vertigo syndrome.

After I had started in Air Traffic Control, on rest days, I continued to do the odd test flight (checking radio equipment) and even partook in a charter flight to Norway, in a Dakota. On this trip my phobia became more pronounced. Ultimately I had to accept that it was no use fighting against it. Initially, as there did not seem any rhyme or reason why I should feel this way, I mentioned my problem to the doctor who gave me my annual ATCO licence medical. He, apart from being a CAA approved medical examiner, was involved with NASA. In his dealings with the American Space Agency, he met some astronauts who suffered similar problems. He said it could be cured but, as I was no longer committed to being airborne, why not just accept that my flying days were over. These words of comfort overcame my initial disgust with myself; in as much as I felt a bit of a fraud, considering all the flying I had done.

This fear of mine, in later years, did not go down too well with the family, as it put paid to holidays by air abroad. I was all right Jack, I had been abroad! Not an attitude I was proud of. Bless them though, once they realised my phobia was genuine, they accepted the fact.

Yet another very valid reason for opting out of the flying game and entering the world of Air Traffic Control was, in time, I was to become a father of two young children. For their future, and Bette's and mine, a job on TERRA FIRMA seemed to me the best bet to overcome my predicament and, at the same time, ensure a more secured environment for their up-bringing.

Not long after I joined ATC and thirteen months after the birth of our son, I was blessed with the arrival of a daughter, Wendy Suzanne. I had always said that if I were going to have a family, my ideal would be to have a son and daughter. Another ambition achieved, with the help of my wife!

Wendy too got the aviation bug later on, like the rest of the family. In fact, on reaching employment age she applied for a job within the Airport Administration. Unfortunately though, due to my status as the Senior Air Traffic Control Officer, at that time in my career, company policy precluded anyone with family connections being employed so, it would be a number of years before her aviation career 'Took-off', as mentioned later on in this narrative.

Now to the mainstay of my career, which spanned 38 years, the description of which occupies most of my story. Albeit, it was largely a static number, compared to the variety of my flying days and therefore, possibly less interesting.

I'll leave that, to whoever reads this saga, to judge for themselves.

4   A New Career

Early Days – 1957

Throughout my career in Air Traffic Control it is important to note the era I refer to hence the reason why each phase, of my involvement, is headed by the relevant year(s). I have done this purely as an indication of how my experiences compare to present day methods of ATC. Hopefully, whoever reads this, will find these reminisce of interest.

Why did I consider ATC as a career, now that my flying days was over? I could have stayed with Skyways on the ground side, as an Operations Officer but being relegated, to flying a desk, didn't appeal to me, quite apart from the other reasons I have outlined earlier.

Some of my contemporaries even opted out of the aviation scene altogether and, in due course, ended up as Publican's. Excepting the social life such a livelihood generates, the long hours and hard work didn't appeal to me. Remember, having lived in one for five years, I knew what was involved.

On the other hand, ATC seemed to be an ideal way of keeping myself involved in the aviation scene without risking my neck in the flying game.

Admittedly, my initial perception of ATC was a trifle short sighted. My imagination ran away with me what I thought would be an ideal way of earning a living. That being, closeted in a Control Tower, looking at different types of aircraft and, occasionally having a 'chat' with them! I am, after all, basically a lazy person so, what better than a sedentary occupation, with the added interest already indicated, thrown in for good measure. In fact, since my first interest in aviation was aroused, aircraft have fascinated me as, indeed, anything mechanical such as steam trains and ships, excepting sailing ones.

I very soon found out that ATC was far more complex than I had imagined. The following pages will amply demonstrate what I mean.

I had, during my flying career, on behalf of the majority of pilots I flew with, carried out a lot of voice communications with ATC, one of my duties as a R/O. However, apart from acknowledging ATC instructions, which were the pilot's responsibility to comply with anyway, I was not all that familiar with the service provided to us aviators.

In due course I was enlightened as to the true nature of ATC thereby dispelling any notions that I may have had, that it would be an easy number to entertain.

Before I could be accepted, I had to attend an interview board, which contained an impressive array of distinguished-looking personnel, which included a female psychologist.

One of the questions they asked, which always amused me, was "Why did you want to come into ATC?" I would have thought the answer was obvious otherwise as, why else would I apply for the job in the first place! On reflection, I suppose this was to safeguard against those individuals who apply for anything, just for the hell of it. The next question was "What would I do if I wasn't accepted?" I must have satisfied their probing questions, and impressed the Board members that, come hell or high water, I was determined to get into ATC one way or another. I was duly accepted, being within the age limit (35) of prospective candidates. My new employer was the then Ministry of Transport and Civil Aviation (MTCA). In other words, I became a civil servant. Hopefully though, without the tea-swilling image those civil servants are noted for. Come to think of it, I did quaff quite a lot of tea!

1957 was the year I started a career, which would span 38 years of my life, and, truthfully I can say, never did I regret the day I was accepted as a suitable ATC candidate.

The first year in my new career was very much a learning process, starting off with a nine-week course at the School of ATC at Hurn Airport, Bournemouth. The school buildings were a collection of wooden huts reminiscent of wartime days. Very basic but they served their purpose. Nowadays, it is a purpose built complex, as befits its status as the College of ATC.

For the duration of this course, I installed my wife and baby son, in a small hotel in Bournemouth, whose main clientele were well to do retired folk. One or two other members of our Primary course (as it was known) also installed themselves in the same residence. Two of my fellow students I can remember, namely John Timpson (I have a photograph of him pushing my son in a pram!) who ultimately rose to the dizzy heights of an ATC Inspector. The second person I remember was Dave Coulson who equally rose, in time, to prominence as the Senior Air Traffic Controller (SATCO for short) of East Midlands Airport. Just as I did when I eventually became SATCO at Blackpool Airport. I mention these facts, in passing, purely as an indication of the calibre of our intake!

I, unlike some of my colleagues, was fortunate in having a car, so I was able to ferry some of them, to and fro from HURN which was poorly served by public transport.

As mentioned earlier, the duration of the course, all 9 weeks of it, was all too little time to absorb all that was thrown at us. It was like being back at school although, this time, we were being paid handsomely for our studies. The subjects covered were contained within numerous documents – what I like to term the academic aspect of ATC – the most important of which were the following. The Manual of Air Traffic Control (MATC), being the controller's 'Bible' throughout his career, and the Air Navigation Order & Rules of the Air and Air Traffic Control. Each student had his own library of documents with the added 'delights' of amendments, additions, deletions, etc, to keep our documents current. Some of the contents needed detailed study whilst, others were more of a reference nature. An exercise in itself. In addition to class room instruction – nine to five office hours with one hour lunch break. It was necessary to spend a couple of hours each evening, during the week, to keep on top of all the lectures our instructors had bombarded us with during school hours. Here, having my wife and son with me, in other words being blessed with my own home comforts on tap, proved to be a big bonus in counteracting the constant 'head in the book' existence we seemed to be subjected to. The choice of life-style I had opted for whilst on this course seemed to me to be infinitely preferable to the alternative which, I suspect would have degenerated into propping up the bar most nights! No doubt others, away from their homes, thought it was a good way of relaxing after their evening studies. My wife helped me a lot in quizzing me on those academic subjects whereby, for examination purposes, one had to be word perfect – parrot fashion – even if one 'did' not understand their meaning. One worked that one out later, when the brain could absorb the meaning of the written word.

At regular intervals, there were progress tests to ensure we were up to date with our studies. They, if nothing else, kept us on our toes.

The academic aspect i.e. the rules and regulations that govern our profession, were well and truly imprinted upon our minds. It was a continuing process that occupied most of our time on this course.

One of the documents that we had to know about, albeit concentrated study of its contents was not required, was the body that looked after civil aviation worldwide. It was known as the International Civil Aviation Organisation (ICAO) based in Montreal, Canada. This organisations prime responsibility was to institute what was known as 'Standard and Recommended Practices'. In plain language, its directives ensured that foreign aircraft operating into our country and, conversely British or any other nationality aircraft, operating in airspace not of their origin, are controlled by the same guidelines, irrespective of whose airspace the relevant aircraft is flying over.

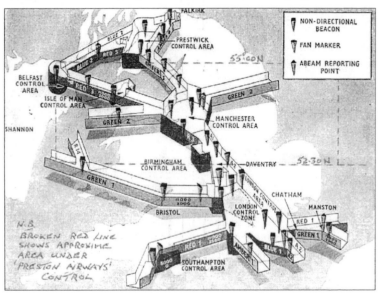

Leaving aside this part of our studies and, before discussing the practical side of our course, a description of how the U.K. airspace is constructed, is worth a mention. In this country there are three Flight Information Regions (FIR's) in which there are aerial corridors, known as AIRWAYS – not unlike the motorway network, lettered and numbered in a similar manner – plus Control Zones situated around the major airports. Other kinds of controlled airspace are also incorporated. The Airways are 10nautical miles wide and extend from a given height above ground, up to a specified altitude (in my day 25,000 feet). Outside controlled airspace is what is known as the open FIR where aircraft can operate without undue interference from ATC. The best way to illustrate what I am trying to describe is by looking at the accompanying map, which I photocopied from an old Encyclopedia book I have in my possession. Incidentally, this map bears little resemblance to the current one; how times have changed!

At a latter stage in the narrative I will explain, in more detail, how ATC operates within these FIR's. For the moment though, a brief description of the difference between the two types of airspace, should suffice.

In controlled airspace, aircraft have to be suitably equipped, and their pilots licenced to a certain standard, to enable them to participate in the ATC service provided. Outside controlled airspace, ATC provides a Flight Information Service (FIS). These areas enable the many private pilots, club aviators and kindred spirits, to enjoy the freedom of the skies, without having to comply with ATC instructions, which is mandatory in controlled airspace. Nevertheless, whilst flying within these areas, certain rules need to be observed in the absence of positive control, to safeguard their activities, albeit the majority of this kind of activity is conducted under what is known as Visual Flight Rules (VFR) – this term will be explained later – in other words, the see and be seen avoidance scenario. Lets face it, the size of the U.K. gives little manoeuvring room for the pleasure flying fraternity and those not yet qualified to participate in the positive controlled environment. ATC, in addition to its more usual role of controlling, provides an alerting service, which covers all classes of airspace, in the event of accidents, emergencies and other mishaps. Major accidents/incidents occurring in remote or sparsely populated areas, such as the Scottish Highlands, Welsh Mountains, the Pennines and off-shore areas, where location could be a problem, the Search and Rescue facilities of the two R.A.F. co-ordination centres (RCCs) covering the U.K. – based at Mount-batten Plymouth and, Pitreavie Edinburgh – would be brought into play.

The ATC authority in whose area the incident occurred would deal with other accidents/incidents. In all cases, civil, and when required the Military, emergency services are fully utilised.

To wind up this part of the exercise, what is the real purpose of ATC? Simply speaking, it is purely a device to prevent collisions between aircraft in the air and those on the ground. How this is achieved will be gone into in more detail as the picture of activities unfolds. As an interim, ATC's motto will give some idea of why ATC is necessary in the first place. Its aim is to ensure a safe, expeditious and orderly flow of traffic: -

Safe   Prevention of collision(s) between aircraft in the air and on the ground.

Expeditious Keeping aircraft moving without undue restriction.

Orderly   Smooth procession of aircraft from one point to another.

Back to our education and the thing that always intrigued me, until I was duly enlightened, as to how controllers were able to keep a picture of all the aircraft they were responsible for, at any given moment of time.

I like to think, of this aspect of ATC as a 'Pictorial Presentation' or, if you like, what constituted the main tools of our trade. Every aircraft was literally represented by a piece of paper of defined length and width – shades of wartime WINDOW come to mind – known as Flight Progress Strips (FPSs). These strips came in blank bundles upon which aircraft details such as call-sign, type, airspeed, height, aerodrome of departure and destination, and other pertinent information, was hand written, usually by Air Traffic Control Assistants (ATCAs) before being passed onto the controller, who was going to have to deal with it, when it entered his airspace of responsibility. This format, I was told, originated in the USA. These strips even came in different coloured bundles to denote to the controller whether he was dealing with en-route traffic, aerodrome departing and arriving traffic, local flights and over flying aircraft.

The FPSs were slotted into grooved holders, with cut-outs underneath, so that they could slide up and down metal runners inserted in purpose built Flight Progress Boards (FPBs). A simple analogy can be drawn in connection with this presentation. Take a length of railway track, turn it upside down, substitute the sleepers for moveable FPS holders, and the rail line corresponds to the metal runners in the FPB.

As a flight progresses through his airspace, the controller will annotate the FPS with his instructions, using internationally recognised symbols – a form of hieroglyphics. When the strip is no longer required, it can simply be withdrawn from its holder and replaced by the next item (aircraft) waiting to be processed. This format is common to all ATC establishments, be they Control Towers, Airways Centres, Control Zones or any other ATC unit.

To me, a novice to the game, this kind of presentation was quite an eye-opener and, once I had got used to it, I must admit it seemed the most logical way of presenting aircraft information to ATC. Incidentally, there were invariably more than one FPB in any one ATC unit therefore, not only could one slide the FPS holders about but, they could also be moved manually from one board to another.

On a potentially hazardous note, originally the FPS holders were of metal construction and, consequently, in the hands of a frustrated controller, they could be a lethal weapon, if he chose to sling it around the control room. It has been known to happen, so I'm told! For safety's sake then and everybody's peace of mind, someone, in their wisdom, decided plastic or rubber holders would be preferable, and so they were instituted. This decision didn't affect the Flight Progress Boards as they were already built into the control consoles, so they were safe from deranged controllers!

What about communications? Voice – VHF R/T – was now the sole means by which aircraft communicated with ATC and, likewise ATC with aircraft. The days of Wireless Telegraphy (W/T) had long ceased, apart from remote areas in so-called third world countries. English is the number one aviation language, world wide, French being secondary. Standard laid down phraseology, in conjunction with the phonetic alphabet, is the most common form of communication. It can be supplemented by plain language, if circumstances warrant clarification of instructions or, misunderstood messages.

Having given some background information on the ATC set-up as a whole, let's return to the classroom for the practical aspect of the Primary course.

Approach Control and Aerodrome Control are inter-linked control functions, which at this stage of our training, was principally all we had to know from a controlling point of view. For the purpose of our training exercises, described shortly, all aircraft are treated as Instrument Flight Rules (IFR) flights; again, this term will be explained more fully later on. Arriving aircraft, under Approach Control, are cleared to a facility, usually a non-directional beacon (NDB) before establishing themselves on an inbound Instrument Landing Aid. Once established, they are transferred to Aerodrome Control for landing clearance and taxiing instructions after landing.

Conversely, departing aircraft are transferred to Approach (APC) control, once they are airborne and climbing away from the vicinity of the aerodrome.

Approach Control is responsible for separating arriving and departing aircraft, within a certain radius of the aerodrome. Aerodrome Control (ADC) takes care of taxiing aircraft, take-off and landing clearances, and issuing en-route ATC instructions where appropriate. ADC is also responsible for preventing accidents between aircraft and other obstacles such as airport vehicles wandering about on the ground,

A simulator room was set aside for practical training 'Aircraft' were 'piloted' by ATCAs hidden in a back room, supposedly for realism!

Our instructors monitored our performances and tested us at regular intervals. For our 'enjoyment', you wouldn't believe the devious scheme they devised to test our capabilities. I'm sure some of them took a great delight in trying to find out our 'breaking point'. All very interesting, but what happens when we come to the real thing, we would find out in due course, no doubt.

Two semi academic subjects that I have omitted to mention are Navigation and Meteorology. During my flying career I took a passing interest in meteorology: particularly when route forecasts indicated a rough ride. Navigation, on the other hand, I hadn't a clue. Why ATC included this subject in their curriculum, I am at a loss to understand, as it never really entered into the equation in our subsequent controlling duties. Nevertheless, I had to learn about its mysteries, so it was a question of starting from scratch.

There was an amusing sequel, which took place, when I sat for the 'end of term' plotting part of the navigation: exam. I was flanked by a former pilot, on one side, and an ex navigator, on the other. Without the exam invigilator noticing, they nudged me every-time they could see I was on the wrong track, our plotting tables were that close. The upshot of this 'arrangement' enabled me to come out on top when the results came out! As for Meteorology, it was a difficult subject. I only managed to scrape through with a pass mark, at the end of the day.

As I am nearing the end of my description of the first stage of my ATC training, I think it would be remiss of me if I didn't justify the reasons I felt it was necessary to go into such detail of what was involved.

I am aware there are books which describe the workings of ATC. I have seen them in Public Libraries. So, inevitably the question arises as to why I am repeating what professional authors have already written. My answer to such an accusation is, if such be the case, is that my description is purely an indication of how much I, and my colleagues, had to learn in the short space of time allotted to us. ATC proved to be considerably more complex than we had imagined. To the majority of us, we were entering into an entirely new aspect of the aviation world. Any ideas we may have had of it being a 'soft option' way of earning a living were soon dispelled. Another reason, for going on at length, is that I suspect modern day training, bears little resemblance to what we were subjected to and therefore maybe my experiences could be of interest to modern day ATC personnel.

Once the Primary course had been completed, the next stage of our training would be carried out at two out-stations, real live aerodromes, the objective being to put classroom exercises into real live situations. This period would take care of the remainder of our year long training stint.

In passing, I know my better half was glad our stay in Bournemouth was almost over as during weekdays, whilst I was at school, she pushed our son endlessly around Bournemouth, in his pram. Not exactly a flat place for such exertions either. On the other hand, bearing in mind that most of our hotel residents were elderly, they did make my wife and son most welcome and entertained them in their own way. Weekends, whilst on the course, we could relax as a family.

Practical Training Phase – U/T Manchester 1957

After a period of leave to unwind and collect my thoughts following an intensive course of instruction, I was detached to the first of my two out-stations, that being Manchester Ringway, now Manchester International Airport.

As it was too far to commute from my home, I installed myself in digs, not far from the airport. My detachment was for three months. On average I spent five days out of seven, away from home.

I was a little bit surprised at the venue in which I was to take part in 'live' controlling. Manchester, after all, was a major airport so; it seemed to me that I was being thrown in at the deep end!

The type of traffic Manchester enjoyed was, I recollect, 95% airline orientated, the remaining 5% club/private flying activity. So, as near as dammit, it was a case of professionals dealing with like personnel, and I was only a U/T professional! The first couple of weeks or so were spent familiarising myself, getting one's bearings, on the airport's physical layout and its immediate surroundings. Amongst other things, even if it is stating the obvious, no two aerodromes are alike, therefore of necessity each aerodrome has its own ATC procedures, to link up with adjacent controlling units. These 'local procedures' form an extension of the controller's 'Bible', the Manual of ATC mentioned previously. Yet more book work to absorb. Once one was judged competent, a certificate of proficiency was issued enabling one to control aircraft, under supervision.

My first taste of the 'hot' seat was a bit awe inspiring. Much to my surprise though I seemed to settle in reasonably quickly. No doubt, my previous aircrew experience, of communicating with ATC, overcame any qualms I might have had. Now my operating role had been reversed i.e. as a controller talking to aircraft, compared with my previous role as a Radio Operator talking to ATC.

Talking of which, I noticed an unusual trait amongst some of my colleagues, in as much as, when they were confronted with a live situation, all of a sudden they became microphone shy. Again, my recent aircrew experience helped me to acclimatise myself in this new aviation environment.

Strangely enough, I can only recall two significant episodes that occurred whilst I was at Manchester. The first one certainly boosted my confidence; the second one made me wonder, momentarily, whether I had chosen the right profession! Let me explain.

As I was still a novice, all my actions were closely monitored by whoever was on duty as the Watch Supervisor. On this particular occasion my supervisor, by the name of Turner (I have forgotten his Christian name although we were on first name terms) was on duty early one morning with me. The traffic situation, at this time of the morning, was such that a stream of departing aircraft, interspersed by the occasional arrival confronted us. I should point out that the majority of these movements were what is known as Instrument Departures and Arrivals. If memory serves me right, the weather conditions on this particular morning, certainly warranted instrument flying by the aircraft pilots, and instrument procedures conducted by ATC. With little or no prompting from my supervisor, I managed to sort this lot out in accordance with ATC's motto. My mentor appeared to be impressed with my performance and, I must admit, it surely augured well for my future in this game.

I was fortunate with most of the supervisors who monitored my progress, as, with one exception, under their tuition I seemed to be taking to this job like a duck to water. The one exception was a gentleman who, fortunately for me, never crossed my path again whilst I was at Manchester. Let me elaborate.

On my off duty days I still did the odd flight, when a R/O was required. On this particular trip, I was on board a Dakota inbound to Manchester from Oslo. On contacting Manchester, I took exception to the tone of the controller's voice, as he issued his instructions. My skipper and his co-pilot thought likewise. He sounded very officious, acting as though he was a policeman of the air. In other words, his R/T conduct indicated a policy of 'do as you are told or else' kind of attitude. If there is one thing I deplore in this game, it is this mental outlook. It is an unfortunate fact of life that, some of our brethren do look upon their ATC role as being policemen of the skies. Even at this early stage of my career, I had very strong views on what I had just experienced. Anyway, to complete this saga, on leaving the aircraft I, in all innocence, stormed into the control tower demanding to know who this officious person was. I was duly confronted with the aforementioned supervisor and to put it mildly, we had words. Hence my previously stated comment of wondering whether I had done the right thing in opting for a career in ATC. Fortunately, common sense prevailed and, realising I had overstepped the mark, I apologised for my outburst. As time went by I was to find this attitude was the exception rather than the rule.

I preferred to think of ATC as being a service industry. I do accept, however, that rules and regulations are necessary to ensure aircraft operate in a safe environment. It's the way a controller performs that makes or mars our reputation as guardians of the skies.

For the remainder of my stay, at Manchester, there is nothing further of note that I can recall.

It had been a highly illuminating introduction to the world of ATC. On reflection, despite my comments about the 'Deep-End' at the beginning, I valued the opportunity of testing my skills at a major airport. The experience I had enjoyed and its attendant benefits at being allowed to perform at such a venue would stay with me throughout my career.

My original perception of ATC was amply rewarded as I can think of no better place, with the possible exception of Heathrow Airport, of being able to see the majority of the world's Airlines, with their varied mix of aircraft types, passing in front of one's very eyes.

Second Out-Station – Blackpool 1957-1958

This detachment was right up my street as I lived virtually on the doorstep. My back garden wall formed part of the aerodrome boundary. Between this wall, and the control tower, I walked between two hangars and, three minutes later; I was at the tower. If the weather was inclement, naturally I took the car!

This aerodrome bore little comparison to Manchester, both from a manpower, and facilities, point of view, not forgetting an entirely different traffic situation. ATC, complement wise, there were no supervisors at Blackpool. One was entirely at the mercy of the ATCO, as they were known in those days and two qualified controllers. There was another u/t controller with me and again, fortune favoured yours truly. Why, one may ask? As it happened, during my flying career, I did fly into and out of this aerodrome quite frequently and, consequently, I had gained a favourable reputation. This must have filtered through to ATC so, presumably, my Boss was being politic in his attitude towards me, which certainly did me no harm. The other student was not favoured in the same way. He'd obviously drawn the short straw.

I spent approximately six months at Blackpool. What a totally different set-up, traffic wise, compared to Manchester. In fact, the ratio of the type of traffic accommodated was inversely proportional. This time I was faced with 90% club/private flying activity, the remaining 10%, or thereabouts, was taken care of by the resident Airline plying forwards and backwards to the Isle of Man and Belfast. The odd charter was thrown in for good measure. Additionally, to make life more interesting, we had to put up with Gliding and Parachuting activity. Admittedly the latter types of operations were controlled by Air Traffic Control Assistants (ATCAs) ensconced in a 'runway control van' situated adjacent the runway in use. Nevertheless, the controller, in the tower, was ultimately responsible for decisions taken by the ATCAs.

An unusual type of activity we enjoyed was a Jet test-flying programme. The Hawker Hunter was being manufactured on the Northeast boundary of the aerodrome. Completed aircraft were regularly test flown from a purpose built runway constructed in 1952. This runway was considerably longer than the original main runway and, of note, Blackpool enjoyed the unique position of being the only aerodrome in the country, at that time, having four tarmac runways.

With reference to these test flights, as there was no radar or ILS system to bring aircraft in during bad weather, I was introduced to an ATC controlling exercise that I hadn't come across before. This procedure enabled these test flights to be conducted irrespective of the weather factor. It was known as the QGH procedure (a descent through cloud for a visual landing). I must confess that, as this was a controller, rather than a pilot, interpreted landing aid and, the fact that I had not been taught how to conduct such an approach, meant it did take me sometime to master it. The idea was to bring the aircraft overhead the aerodrome, descend it to a timed distance and track outbound, before bringing it back on a reciprocal track for a visual landing. All this procedure was based entirely upon Direction Finding (D/F) bearings, and the controller's interpretation of them, enabling the aircraft to land safely after its sortie. My boss was a past master at this unusual ATC procedure and, thanks to his persistent patience, I eventually got the hang of it. It was however to be one of the few aspects of my controlling duties that I never really felt at home with. Many years later, when I was the boss, I actually fought against its use as, by then, we had talk-down radar, a more precise landing aid and more satisfying to operate.

Yet another form of control, not experienced before, was the question of dealing with non-radio equipped aircraft. Blackpool was blessed with quite a lot of this type of activity. Fortunately the use of Aldis Lamp signals, was an item on the Primary Course agenda, so we were prepared. Additionally, for this type of traffic a signals square was situated in front of the control tower.

The mix of radio and non-radio equipped aircraft, from a controlling point of view, tested one's abilities no end. It was akin to being a 'one armed paper hanger', what with speaking into the microphone with one hand, and operating the Aldis lamp, with the other, if there was no one around to assist you. All that was needed to complete the illusion that you were in control of the situation was to have a set of semaphore flags as back up!

Due to the predominant nature of the type of flyer we had to contend with at Blackpool, they being club and private aviators, out tuition was largely centred around Aerodrome control, and all that entails. For example, taxiing patterns (routes), take-off and landing clearances, circuit details, off circuit flying, etc., occupied most of our time, in this particular phase of practical controlling. Approach control, comparatively speaking, was not one of our widely used procedures. Nevertheless the 'Separation Standards' that had been drummed into us on the Primary course, came in very useful on those occasions when separation of IFR traffic became necessary.

At this juncture, a word or two on the basic principles that govern civil flying is, I think, appropriate. There are two disciplines, irrespective of the type of airspace involved, that govern the conduct of flights. They are Instrument Flight Rules (IFR) and Visual Flight Rules (VFR). The former discipline largely governed Manchester's type of traffic whilst the latter, was very much predominant at Blackpool. Another comparison is worth a mention in that, whereas at Manchester, I had been used to dealing almost exclusively with professional pilots, now it was the turn of the ab-initio, club students, low flying hour private pilots and the like, who exercised our skills in controlling them. As in all walks of life, one has to start from scratch and therefore, inevitably, mistakes occur. Controllers faced with this type of aviation activity, particularly trainees like myself, had to be extra vigilant in the performance of their duties. The time honoured expression 'Patience is a virtue' was particularly applicable at a place like Blackpool, if you wished to assert your authority, without being too dictatorial.

Referring back to the two disciplines mentioned earlier, I found, dealing with IFR traffic, was more straightforward, in as much that those on both 'sides of the fence' i.e. Pilots and Controllers, were used to complying with and issuing instructions, with little or no ambiguity involved.

VFR traffic however was rather a different story. The majority of pilots, who operated under this banner, required little control, except when flying within the aerodrome circuit. Outside the boundaries of the Aerodrome Traffic Zone (ATZ), a definition of this type of ATC airspace appears later on, these types of pilots were responsible for maintaining their own separation from other aircraft. In these circumstances, ATC provided an information service only. Not unlike the FIR controller's terms of reference, also explained later on.

The interesting part of a controller's life at a place like Blackpool, particularly in the early stages, was the interrogation of IFR and VFR traffic situations. For the moment though, I will refrain from detailing with how we resolved such problems, until such time I became a fully fledged licensed controller, with some background experience to fall back on.

Suffice to say that the practical trainee periods I experienced gave me a very broad outlook on the problems that faced me in my new profession. In fact, I would venture to say that my training curriculum, at two dissimilar venues, more than covered the ATC spectrum. I consider myself fortunate in the choice of aerodromes I had been detached to, for training purposes.

The culmination of the practical training period resulted in a return to the School of ATC, to take the final examination for my ATCOs licence, more commonly known as the 'Yellow Peril'. Indeed, the binder incorporating the licence was yellow in colour.

In my day, there was no formality in being presented with your licence. As I remember, it was just handed to you on successful completion of the examination. Nowadays, the licence presentation ceremony is quite an occasion, not unlike a university graduation day.

I returned to Blackpool and actually operated solo for a month or so, before being whisked away on another course of instruction at the School of ATC, this time to be taught the intricacies of working at an Airways Centre.

Yet another rating (Airways A) to add to the ones already annotated in my licence, those being Aerodrome and Approach Control Ratings. Before proceeding further, a word about the rating system is, I think, appropriate. A controller's licence is annotated by ratings according to the specific ATC function he will perform.

Initially, in my era, on receiving your licence, the Aerodrome and Approach ratings were inscribed. These two ratings could be separate

ATC functions, as in the case of Manchester, or combined, as in the case of Blackpool. The nature of the facilities, staffing, and status of a particular aerodrome determined how the Approach and Aerodrome functions would be conducted.

One further point is that each rating had to be validated at the ATC unit one had been assigned to, before a controller could operate solo.

Airways Course – Early 1958

Back to school! I thought my education days were over. However, as this further schooling was to enhance my status as a controller, why should I complain? Incidentally I was accompanied by my ex ATCO I/C, one George Dickenson, who would be trained as a 'D' man.

I forget the duration of this course or anything of note worth recording. So, with out further a do, a brief description of what it entailed, should be sufficient. There were two types of controllers employed in Airways Centres, namely 'D' men, who did the actual controlling, and 'A' men who fed the 'D' men, via the FPS format, with all the information the latter required, to carry out his controlling duties. This course was much more of a practical nature, compared to the Primary one and therefore, in my eyes, more interesting.

As 'A' men, which I was) my colleagues and I were, to all intents and purposes, strip 'bashers'. Glorified assistants if you like, no disrespect to our ATCA brethren intended.

The following illustration of what went on in this course should give the reader some idea of what it was all about.

For training purposes, everything was done on a simulation basis. A classroom was set up to represent an Airways Centre.

A brief description of an Airways Centre system is necessary here, to paint a replica picture. Airway corridors are delineated throughout their length by radio beacons, known as reporting points. They are spaced at geographical positions (see map on page 48) for ease of identification. As traffic transits from one beacon to the next, our task as 'A' men was to calculate, using pre-computed tables, the times an aircraft would over-fly a particular reporting point. This information, in conjunction with pilot's reports as they cross these aerial signposts, was vitally important to the 'D' men. It was the only method by which he could picture and control his traffic. Each aircraft of course was represented by a separate FPS. The testing of a 'D' man's controlling skills came to the fore when dealing with the following separation of aircraft scenarios: -

1. Opposite direction traffic climbing/descending through other aircraft's heights.

2. Maintaining vertical separation between aircraft – a minimum of 1000 feet.

3. Longitudinal separation i.e. time differential between aircraft flying at the same height and in the same direction; 10 minutes between identical aircraft types; shorter time if leading aircraft is so many knots faster than the succeeding one(s); greater time if the roles are reversed, depending upon the relative speeds of the aircraft concerned.

4. Route variation, being either geographical or diverging flight paths. In short, in all the foregoing scenario's, the 'D' man's priority was to ensure that NO two aircraft appeared over the same reporting point at the same time and at the same height.

For realism purposes, as in the Primary course, 'aircraft' were 'piloted' by ATCAs on the simulator.

On reflection, this course inevitably concentrated more on the training of the 'D' men than us 'A' men. After all, it's the former persons who would have the responsibility of controlling real live aircraft. As 'A' men, my colleagues, and I took no part in actual controlling. At this stage of my career I don't think I could have coped with such intricate controlling, hence the reason why only senior controller grades were tasked as 'D' men. I was content with the role I had been programmed for, not that I had much option!

In the real world, scheduled Airlines were the main users of this type of airspace, as it ensured them protection throughout their flight. Major aerodromes, such as Heathrow, Manchester and Prestwick for example, also had their own portions of controlled airspace, in the form of 'stubs' which protruded into the airways system (again refer to previous map) which added protection for the airlines in the take-off and landing phases of their flight paths.

The instructors on this course, similar to the ones I enjoyed on the Primary course, also had field days in devising all manner of simulated exercises, including emergencies, to test the budding 'D' men. To my inexperienced eye, what these controllers were put through, was mind boggling. No wonder the odd 'D' man had his work cut out to master the intricacies of such an involved controlling complex.

It appeared to me and I suspect others, that airways control, London in particular, was probably the most demanding ATC task imposed upon any controller.

Of note, although us 'A' men wouldn't be involved in actual controlling, the importance of knowing the ATC procedural separation standards, could not be underestimated, a factor that was to benefit me later on in my career. When I became an aerodrome controller, the application of these standards became the 'norm', in separating IFR traffic at an aerodrome.

The only time, in the foreseeable future, that I would actually 'talk' to an aircraft would be when I performed FIR controlling duties, at the Airways Centre I was destined for. The majority of our time, on this course, was spent on simulator exercises. I won't bore the reader any more except to say time was drawing near whereby 'make-believe' would be replaced with reality.

My posting to an Airways Centre was imminent.

Preston Airways – 1958-1962

A few miles north of Preston, just off the A6 road leading towards Lancaster and the Lake District, there stood on a small hill, just off the main road, what looked like a country mansion which I was told it once was.

This was to be my work place for the next four years, interrupted mid-way by attending an Area Radar Course, more of that later, and the odd relief controlling stint at Blackpool.

This establishment went by the name of Barton Hall, which housed the Northern Air Traffic Control Centre; known to all and sundry as Preston Airways.

The actual control room was situated in what was once the courtyard. As protection from the elements, a glass-panelled roof had been constructed atop.

Other parts of the building contained Administration Offices, PBX and teleprinter rooms, Meteorological Office, Radio Workshops, etc, not forgetting private accommodation for the overall Superintendent in charge of this lot. There was even a detachment of R.A.F. personnel who manned what was known as the Distress and Diversion cell (D&D) for aircraft missing, or in trouble. They also controlled Military aircraft operating within the Preston FIR. In other words, this centre was a joint Civil and Military set-up.

As an annex to the main building, there was wooden hut accommodation occupied, in the main, by those members of staff who lived too far away from their homesteads. For these people, their leisure activities were accommodated in another wooden hut which was turned into a bar, cafeteria and games room. Us control personnel were not averse to taking advantage of these facilities, watch-keeping duties permitting. For myself, I was able to commute daily from my home.

This centre was a 24-hour operation, 7 days a week, 365 days a year including Christmas day. For the first time in my life I had to contend with all night shifts, apart from those experienced during my flying days. To begin with they were novel but that soon wore off. I never really took to night work as, apart from anything else, like many others I suspect, it upset my body clock. For the time being though, I had no option but to grin and bear it. Whilst on this subject, it is worth pointing out that a controller's life is governed by shift patterns, more commonly known as Watches. There can be some very anti-social hours involved, so if you are looking for a nine to five number in life, forget it, this is no profession for you! Before describing the control room complex and what our duties consisted of, a broad picture of the airspace Preston FIR occupied, is worth noting. Looking at the map on a previous page, the Preston FIR was sandwiched between the London and Scottish FIR's. Within this region there was the system of airways and control zones surrounding the major airports, also seen on the map. The FIR boundaries corresponded to Latitude 52.30 N in the South, Daventry being the main geographical controlled airspace entry/exit point for the main North/South airway (Amber 1), and Latitude 55.00 N in the North, Deancross, not marked on the map, being the equivalent Northern controlled airspace entry/exit point, for the same airway. The West and East longitudinal boundaries (I cannot remember the exact longitudes) approximated to mid Irish Sea and mid North Sea.

All aircraft operating within this area, whether flying in (A) controlled airspace, or (B) in the FIR were, in (A's) case, controlled by

Preston Airways and, in (B's) case, they were the responsibility of the Preston FIR service. The only exception being departing and landing traffic at airports within Preston FIR. The individual airport's Approach control facility, looked after inbound landing traffic when released by Preston. Conversely, departing traffic was transferred by Approach control upon it entering the airways system. Off airways traffic communicated with the FIR controller, there being no positive control as such, which I will explain later.

Let me describe, as best I can, the control room layout.

Bearing in mind the supposed origin of Barton Hall, picture for a moment what a Banqueting room in this kind of establishment, would look like. In the centre of such a room, there is usually an elongated dining table complete with chairs. The control room console was not unlike this portrayal, with an added appendage of a Pyramid like structure. In this case though, our Pyramid only had two sloping sides instead of the normal three, associated with such a structure. To complete the picture of the Ops room, as it was generally known, at one end of the room there was a glass fronted enclosed office, occupied by the overall Watch Supervisor. At the other end, tucked away in a corner, sat the FIR controller surrounded by a bevy of female Assistants. Lucky fella!

Now I will describe the operational aspect of what we had been trained for.

Each sloping side of our pyramid structure consisted of banks of FPBs with their attendant FP holders, complete with inserted FPSs. One sloping side was the domain of the 'D' controllers, the opposite side being occupied by their 'A' counterparts. Each side was divided into four sectors, individually manned by a 'D' and 'A' controller. Maybe I am stating the obvious but, again with reference to the map, as more than one airway occupied our airspace, it would be impossible for one man to control all the aircraft, throughout this region. So there is no misunderstanding of what I have tried to describe so far, the 'D' men, as opposed to the FIR controller, is responsible solely for the positive, mandatory control of controlled airspace traffic.

Within the four sectors, on the 'D' side, there were permanently displayed Blocking strip holders denoting the various reporting points, identified by radio beacons, spaced at regular intervals. These enable aircraft to navigate within the confines of the airways corridors, pilots termed this exercise as beacon hopping, and also enable the 'D' men to monitor each aircraft's progress. At the same time, it gave him manoeuvring room to climb and descend aircraft through en-route traffic. Not an easy controlling exercise, as standard procedural separation had to be maintained at all times. In fact, he had to be a mental gymnast to calculate the opportune times that descents and climbs could be accommodated. By contrast, over-flights with no climbs or descends to bother about were easy to deal with. Also permanently displayed on the 'D' side were further blocking strip holders, denoting an airports main entry/exit point; again identified by a radio beacon. To the 'D' man, for inbound landing aircraft to an airport within his sector, this was the clearance limit beyond which the Approach control facility of the relevant airport would take over control. Conversely, departing aircraft entering the airways system were transferred from that airports approach control, to the relevant 'D' controller.

Having given some time to the role of the 'D' men let me now concentrate on my side of the fence. Namely us 'A' men.

Our FP boards were rarely empty of FPSs. Our ATCAs constantly fed us with flight plans of intended flights through our airspace, whereupon we had to complete separate strips for each entry, en-route and exit point denoted by the blocking strips on the 'D' side. Not only that, each flight plan represented a different aircraft, so the whole process was repeated for each and every aircraft partaking in controlled airspace. For those aircraft landing or departing from airports within the Preston FIR, further strips were required for the transfer reporting points i.e. between the airways system, and the relevant airport(s). Most of the time our FP boards were full of pending flights waiting to be activated, before being placed on the 'D' side. Physically, we placed these strip holders on the 'D' side, by leaning over the top of the pyramid structure. We 'A' men had to be agile. 'D' men led a more sedentary life style!

I omitted to mention in describing the physical layout of our operations, that each side of the pyramid had banks of telephones. Additionally on the 'D' side, as they wore headsets for communication purposes, they had plug in jacks with transmit/receive buttons. Consequently, we on the 'A' side were unable to monitor an aircraft's progress. There was a loud speaker system but, because of the noise levels in the control room, it was rarely used.

Another of our chores was to pass aircraft estimates to adjacent airway centres where responsibility for their onward flights rested with the latter centres. Also, where applicable, destination airports within our FIR would be informed of an aircraft's expected time of arrival. Similarly, those airports whose departure aircraft would be entering the airways system, would pass us airborne times so that we could activate the appropriate strips for the 'D' man's operations.

To put all this in perspective, once an aircraft had crossed any of the blocking strip markers, permanently displayed on the 'D' side, be they en-route reporting points, airport entry/exit points, etc, the 'D' man would note the time the aircraft passed over the relevant point, together with any of his instructions, and annotate his FPS accordingly, so that he could plan his onward controlling exercise. The method of time calculation we 'A' men used, between each blocking strip facility, was computed by a set of tables, one to each sector, dependant upon the aircraft's speed together with the wind factor i.e. direction and strength at different height bands.

Upon the return of the FPS from the 'D' side, once the latter had finished with it, an enthusiastic 'A' man would note whether the times, computed and actual, coincided. If they did, it was the hallmark of a conscientious 'A' man's input, not to mention the 'D' man's relief on being able to rely upon his 'A' man's expertise. As we gained experience, the importance of accurate information we fed to the 'D' men, could not be underestimated, easing the workload of the latter gentlemen. In fact, I would go as far to say that the controlling complexities of our 'D' men could be considerably eased by the dedication of the 'A' man's contribution. Our duties might seem to those of us who wanted to be actively involved in controlling, like me, a little on the mundane side, but as no two consecutive days traffic patterns were alike, apart from the daily scheduled flights, one managed to maintain an interest in what was required of us.

Team spirit was essential in the way we carried out our allotted tasks, bearing in mind that one didn't always work with the same 'D' controller. After all, they are individuals, not robots, having their own idiosyncrasies, so the sooner we 'A' men learnt about 'D' men's interpretation of his controlling guidelines, the easier our relationships became.

The efficiency of this ATC unit was demonstrated by the remarkably few near misses, known as 'air-misses', that occurred whilst I was there.

As a break from strip 'bashing', us 'A' men were rostered at regular intervals, to do stints as FIR controllers. Our main responsibility in this sphere of ATC was to warn aircraft about any other aircraft, if they appeared to be in close proximity, as they were not subjected to the constraints of controlled airspace. We also broadcast navigation and meteorological warnings that could be relevant to the safety of their flights. On a couple of occasions, my day was made for me, when two of my old pilot colleagues, on hearing my voice, greeted me like a long lost friend. Nice to know I had not been forgotten.

I welcomed these FIR duties as, at least, I could talk to real live aircraft, even if I couldn't see them. Excepting the occasional personal touch just related, all we were really doing was communicating with disembodied voices. For instance, during practically the whole time I was at Barton Hall, I never saw an aircraft from one day to the next. Not really my idea of how I wanted to be involved in ATC.

Yet another of our duties worth a mention is how night shifts affected our workload.

Naturally the traffic at night tailed off into a trickle, nevertheless we had to prepare for the following mornings 'rush hour' onslaught of scheduled flights. All the relevant details had to be written on fresh blank FPS's, relative to the aircraft that would be flying through our airspace. Consequently, our FP boards resembled a mass of pending activity, which the 'D' men would have to cope with on the morrow. Another chore that required our attention, before we could even consider getting our heads down for a while, was to bundle up all the preceding days used FPSs, there being separate bundles for each reporting point and airport clearance limit designators. These were placed in storage boxes, principally for statistical purposes. These strips had to be retained for a specific period of time, something that was applicable to all ATC units, in the event they might be required as evidence in accident/incident investigations. This was one of the reasons why such emphasis was placed upon accurate strip marking, as each FPS paints a story of an aircraft's progress. Throughout my career, I was very keen on this aspect of our responsibilities, whatever function of ATC I was performing.

To complete the picture of my night shift experiences, towards the end of my stay at Barton Hall, I was occasionally invited to cross the floor, as it were, and operate as a 'D' man, when the traffic situation involved no controlling gymnastics! All done, of course, with the connivance of a friendly 'D' man. Yes, I did have some friends on the other side! No doubt, the powers that be would have frowned upon such unorthodox carry-ons. To me though, it was a welcome break from strip marking.

The first couple of years at Barton Hall, I found this different kind of controlling, and the part we lesser mortals played in it, novel and interesting. Nevertheless, I didn't relish the idea of spending the rest of my natural, in this area of ATC. As luck would have it, this was NOT to be my destiny anyway, as I will explain shortly.

About mid-way through my term in this airways centre, I was sent on an Area Radar course. As there was no radar unit at Barton Hall, the nearest one being a limited converge one at the old RNAS station at Stretton. It seemed to me a bit of a pointless exercise because as far as I was aware, on completing the course, I would return to Barton Hall to resume my 'A' man's duties. Which is exactly what happened. In other words, there was no opportunity to validate my radar rating but, at least, I was able to show another rating inscribed in my licence which, by now, was beginning to look quite an impressive document. Why look a gift horse in the mouth, one may ask! In fact, obtaining this rating did prove beneficial in the long run, when I eventually operated talk-down radar, in my subsequent career at Blackpool Airport. Although the latter was a different type of radar, when it came to operating it, I didn't have to go through the rigmarole of attending another radar course.

After my return to Barton Hall I was detached, on the odd occasion, to Blackpool as a leave and sickness relief controller. This was right up my street, as I felt I was back in the sphere of ATC where I was convinced my future belonged.

During the course of these detachments, rumours were flying around that Blackpool Airport's owners, who were also my employers, the Ministry of Transport and Civil Aviation (MTCA) were considering selling the airport to the local authority, Blackpool Borough Council. In due course, these rumours became fact. I pricked up my ears and awaited developments with interest. In the meantime I carried on with my 'A' man's duties, in the knowledge that my stay at Barton Hall could be of limited duration. I didn't fancy the future of the majority of my colleagues who were destined for airways centres, control zones or, the up and coming radar control centres. Here contact with the outside world of aviation would continue to be a case of talking to disembodied voices, with little chance of seeing who they were dealing with.

The opportunity of controlling at an aerodrome was not to be lightly dismissed. Before committing myself irrevocably, (I had been offered a job at Blackpool under its new ownership), I had to consider seriously the pros and cons of what I proposed to do.

I couldn't escape the fact that I would be giving up a possibly more secure employment number, a decent salary that my new employer could not match and a sizeable pension at the end of the day. On the other hand, the advantages I would gain were as follows. There is no denying I would enjoy a much better ATC environment in relation to job satisfaction. Also, if I could prove my competency and keep my nose clean, I could well step into the shoes of the present ATCO I/C, a gentleman by the name of D.J. Harrison, who had been a Watch Supervisor whilst I was at Barton Hall. He had been detached to Blackpool to see out his twilight years of employment, before compulsory retirement. He only had three years to go. To cut a long story short, I did succeed him in 1965.

Having weighed up what to do for the best, I decided there was no contest. I took my leave of the MTCA and joined the non-state world of ATC. All non MTCA types were dubbed non-state ATCOs except those at contractor run aerodromes. Thanks to the Ministry employing me in the first place, I had enjoyed a memorable innings, not to mention the invaluable experience of being trained by them.

To sum up my experiences whilst employed by the MTCA and, in particular, the length of time I had spent at Barton Hall, is perhaps worth a comment. I acknowledge that what I am about to say would not necessarily be the views of some of my colleagues. I had adopted a philosophy of the importance I attached to ATC/Pilot relationships. In that I am implying that we in ATC had a vital contribution to make in the way pilots conducted their operations and, not least of all, appreciating one another's problems in the safe conduct of flight. Rightly or wrongly, I gained the impression that some of our older controllers, through no fault of their own, didn't always appreciate the workload our pilot colleagues were subjected to when trying to fly their aircraft in accordance with ATC instructions. I suppose these occasional misunderstandings could be put down to the fact that our elders were, in the main, ex wartime aircrew not entirely conversant with modern day aircraft, compared to their wartime basic cockpit layouts and the their lack of ATC. By contrast, I enjoyed the advantage of being one of the very few civilian flyers who entered ATC direct and therefore was more conversant with the workload imposed upon pilots. The complex ATC system controllers were required to master, cannot have been an easy task. Nevertheless due to my background, I tended to sympathise more with what pilots had to put up with, in endeavouring to comply with ATC instructions, rather than give my all to my responsibilities as a controller. I was guilty of this attitude throughout my subsequent ATC career. In the following pages I tend to harp upon my philosophy for which I make no apology.

5   A NEW BEGINNING

Blackpool Airport 1962–1965

A new era in my ATC career was about to begin. The most welcome part of transferring my allegiance was that there would be no more travelling, no more night shifts, not for the time being anyway,

And, most important of all, I would achieve my ambition of working in a control tower on an active aerodrome.

As my new employer was the Local Government Authority, it was a complete change. Apart from some ATCAs who elected to stay on in ATC, staffing had to be arranged. The only controller 'relic' from the MTCA days was the present ATCO I/C – the gentleman I have mentioned previously, who elected to remain in situ until his retirement. If he hadn't elected to stay on, he would have been retired automatically there and then. He was not however the type of person to give up the reigns of ATC just yet. Apart from him and myself, another controller was engaged by the name of Pete Houghton, to make up the minimum controller compliment that our new employer considered adequate to staff the ATC unit. Pete was ex-Hucknall (a contractors aerodrome) and therefore unlike myself, he had some experience of working at an aerodrome. Mine was limited to my supervised stints at Manchester and Blackpool. Being of a similar disposition to myself, I was glad to have him aboard.

I realised, before I had committed myself to local government employment, that staffing wise, it would be on a shoe-string basis, unlike my previous employer who, if anything, tended to overstaff places like Blackpool.

Local government, at this stage of the game, did not recognise ATC as a separate profession. By that I mean there was no provision within local government terms of reference, concerning pay and conditions of service structure. As a result, they tended to vie with one another, airport ownership wise, as to who could get away with minimum staffing levels, at the cheapest rate! The more affluent local authorities were a bit more generous. Blackpool was not in that league. Due to this fact there was a regular turnover of ATC personnel, controllers in particular, which was an on-going feature for a number of years, even after I had become the SATCO. Eventually our union NALGO came to the rescue and devised a common pay and conditions of service structure. This forced local government employers to recognise, after all, that we were a legitimate body of professional men and therefore should be included in their terms of reference as such. Once all-party agreement had been reached on this issue, the turnover of controller personnel, from one venue to another, dropped dramatically.

Anyway... enough of the politics.

I had made my bed and therefore I had to lie in it, not that I regretted opting for this sort of life. In passing, Pete and I initially experienced the shortcomings of our staffing levels, which I will illustrate shortly.

In the meantime, as this airport was to be my 'home' for the next 33 years, a description of our habitat and the role ATC played in its make-up seems appropriate at this stage of the narrative.

The area occupied by the airport was 530 acres. It was situated between the towns of Blackpool and St Annes. It was bounded on the west side by the Irish Sea and to the East Side, inland towards Preston and the Pennines. Some people said the airport was an ideal green belt between the two towns and would have preferred it without the airport. I'm rather glad that the former was the case otherwise, my colleagues, and I would have been out of a job!

What facilities, both from the aviators point of view, and ours in ATC, were on offer?

The airport, in this period of its existence, enjoyed four useable tarmacadam runways with their associated taxiways. In between, there was a sufficient grass area to accommodate gliding and parachuting activity, which was very much a part of the aviation scene at this time in the airport's history.

The other Blackpool Tower, not the airport one, was a well-known recognised landmark situated over two and a half miles north of the airport. Many a pilot has been thankful for this structure, as a means of locating the airport if he hadn't visited us before. Equally, for those flyers that, for one reason or other, had become lost, it was a welcome sight. Apart from being a useful 'aerial signpost', it was the only obstruction of substance, in the height mode, within a twenty mile radius of the airport. Not many airports enjoy such a structure free zone within their vicinity.

The facilities ATC had on offer to assist pilots and help controllers to perform their tasks were, to put it mildly, very limited to begin with. In fact, the only aid pilots had to assist them in locating the airport in adverse weather, was a direction finder, known as VHF/DF. The equipment in the control tower, associated with this facility, consisted of a cathode ray tube (CRT), calibrated in a 360-degree compass rose. Every time an aircraft, or we transmitted, a trace would appear on the CRT enabling pilots to steer a course to locate the airport and controllers to determine the direction the aircraft was coming from, but that was all! This equipment could not give us a range or height of an aircraft.

At this stage, unlike most comparable airports, we didn't have a non-directional beacon (NDB) which would enable pilots to home their aircraft to their airport in the absence of any other radio aid. Sometime after I joined, this shortcoming was rectified. So now we had two facilities of equal benefit to our 'customers' the pilots, as I liked to refer them, and ourselves. We enjoyed, if that's the right term; our fair share of non-radio equipped aircraft, which could be a bit of a pain in the neck controlling wise. For their benefit, a signals square was placed in front of the control tower, indicating the active runway, taxiing pattern, and any other pertinent or restrictive rules that had to be complied with. We, in the tower, controlled non-radio traffic with the aid of an Aldis Lamps, with different coloured filters denoting the instruction(s) we wished to convey.

The tower building was ideally placed, not quite bang in the middle of the airport, but near enough whereby we could survey all our parish of responsibility; they being runways, taxiways, aircraft hard-standings, and the main apron in front of the terminal complex. I favoured this situation in that, unlike many airports, it was not placed immediately adjacent, or on top of, the administrative buildings. In other words we enjoyed splendid isolation away from the prying eyes of our Lords and Masters in the Admin block!

The tower, some wags referred to it as the Ivory tower, was a standard wartime control building, with an all round visual control room (VCR) fixed atop, ATCs domain. The building was two storeys high. The ground floor consisted of a PBX and teleprinter room, incorporating their personnel. Additionally there was a separate kitchen, and toilets facilities. A real bonus, particularly to us in ATC, was a Ministry of Defence Meteorological Office, the only department on the airport not owned or run by the local authority. We enjoyed the advantages of having our own Met Office on our doorstep for many years to come, which meant that unlike the majority of our colleagues at other airports, we controllers did not have to qualify for Met certificates.

The first floor was the radio technician's workshop (formerly the control room in the wartime days) plus a separate office for the Senior ATCO, which in three short years, I was to occupy. Another room, directly below the VCR, eventually became the radar room. All in all, a nice little self-contained complex. In my opinion, a very pleasant environment in which to work.

Now for the nuts and bolts of ATC operations.

The control room console consisted of standard FP boards, clocks, D/F repeater display, airport lighting panel, telephone and R/T jacks, Aldis lamps and, amongst other bits and pieces, the usual library of documents, mainly used as sources of reference. All control towers have their quota of bumf!

The personnel compliment on any one watch was normally one controller and one assistant. The control desk was an L shaped structure, the longer part of the L being the controller's position, the shorter being the assistant's desk.

The functions of Aerodrome and Approach control were combined, so there was only one VHF/RT channel to accommodate both functions.

The presentation format was as described previously. You will recall I mentioned that the FPSs were coloured to indicate the nature of a flight one had to deal with. At Barton Hall most strips were buff or blue coloured, the former colour indicating eastbound flights and the latter colour westbound flights. The buff colour also indicated inbound flights to airports, blue being their departure flights as used at places like Manchester. We at Blackpool, apart from the buff strips for inbound and blue strips for outbound flights, used pink strips due to the predominance of club and private flying activity,. These were in two designs, one of which was for circuit details. The design of this particular strip, enabled controllers to record all take-off and landing times which, in turn, meant he could depart and land traffic in between the circuit 'bashers', a normal circuit taking five minutes, a particularly useful controlling format when the circuit was very active. Some controllers found the mechanics of recording each and every take-off and landing time took a bit of getting used to, but it proved an invaluable method of keeping tabs on one's circuit activities and at the same time, slotting in other traffic, in particular schedules and other non-circuit activity. Of course it must be remembered that all take-off/landing times had to be recorded, irrespective of the nature of the flight and what colour strip one was using. The other pink strip was used for flight which went off on local flights before returning to land with us.

Aerodrome control was our main source of activity. Approach control, due to the comparative lack of IFR traffic to warrant its function, was nevertheless a very important part of our responsibilities, when the need arose.

Before discussing the two principle disciplines of flight, namely VFR and IFR, mentioned previously, and how they affected us in our workload at Blackpool, Pete and I, as previously indicated, started off our working life at this airport with a vengeance. Our boss was the type of person who, although he knew the job like the back of his hand, book wise, was more of an administrative type rather than a practicing controller. He believed in a seven day week attendance, week in and week out but with rare attendance's in the control room itself. As a result, Pete and I ended up doing a seven week stint without a break. Not suprisingly, we thought this was getting beyond a joke! In the end, we had to enlist the services of the Airport Director, to persuade our boss that we were entitled to the odd day off!

Blackpool was to be my first real baptism of fire operationally. Up to now I had been virtually a trainee controller, under supervision. True, at Barton Hall I was operating solo, but as previously indicated, my role there didn't really exercise my potential as a controller. Now I was faced with putting my theoretical knowledge to the practical test, with no one to guide me. I was aware that my peers would judge all my actions, in a competency sense, in particular the professional pilots who would be relying upon my instructions to keep them at a safe distance from other aircraft. The various ways this was achieved will be revealed shortly. We did have a resident airline plying the Isle of Man and Belfast routes. The I.O.M. route, in particular, being very active.

Our main occupation though was looking after flying club activity, private pilots, resident or visiting ones, not forgetting the gliders, which was mainly a weekend activity.

Circuit details, more commonly known as circuits and bumps, and local flying exercises, were the main bread and butter areas of our responsibilities. Here the object of the exercise, from our point of view, was to control and sequence traffic in such a manner that there would be adequate spacing between each aircraft, flying within our allotted airspace, known as the Aerodrome Traffic Zone. This being our little parcel of airspace in which we had overall jurisdiction. Its size was ground level to 2000 feet radius of 2.5nm from the centre of the aerodrome.

One of our responsibilities was to resolve any potential confliction situations, whenever they arose, which they did frequently. In a nutshell then, to try and ensure a safe operation at all times, without being too restrictive or dogmatic.

Not an easy balancing act as I very soon discovered.

Such situations exercised one's controlling skills in no uncertain manner and as in all walks of life, only constant practice and building up experience, would count in the long run. One cannot expect to be the 'ace of the base' immediately after qualifying as a controller. Talking of which, human nature being what it is, occasionally one comes across characters who, the moment they qualified thought they knew it all and to boot, would not listen to advice! In this instance I am referring to a minority of newly qualified private pilots (PPLs), who I came across in the course of my duties. An attitude that personally, I would never ascribe to! One never stops learning in this game, no matter how much experience one has. At a later date, I came across an example of such a person who, nearly every time he got airborne, caused consternation. His antics could almost be described as hilarious, if they were not downright dangerous, I will touch upon his exploits later in the narrative.

Such was the variety and at times, the frequency of traffic we were required to handle, that a years experience in the 'hot seat' was, in my opinion, the bare minimum time one needed, before one could claim mastery of most traffic situations thrown at us. Even then, one could still learn from any unusual occurrences, bearing in mind that no two consecutive days flying programme would be the same. Furthermore, at this early stage of my operational life I would venture to say that my level of experience was not dissimilar to a recently qualified airline pilot having all his academic qualifications but very little flying experience.

In my circumstances I had three years to master my subject before being elevated to being the boss of Blackpool Airport's ATC Unit. This promotion was still very much on the cards. In fact I seem to recall the Airport Director, Jack Jackman, who took over this role under local government ownership, had previously indicated to me that the SATCO's position was mine if I wanted it, upon retirement of D.J. Harrison. When the time came I didn't hesitate to accept this offer.

In one of the previous pages detailing my training stint at Blackpool, I identified the two principle disciplines governing flying activity, namely VFR and IFR flights. These applied irrespective of the nature of a particular flight and aircraft size and type. Albeit the VFR details encompassed, in the main, the smaller types of aircraft flown by flying clubs and private individuals, for example Cessna's, Cherokees, Chipmunks and similar types. VFR flights were also conducted by those pilots who would not or could not take part in a positive control environment, with the exception of Aerodrome Traffic Zones. In any case VFR was not permitted in the airways system, all their aircraft come under the IFR ruling. A further comment concerning VFR is worth noting in as much that such activity is only valid under laid down weather minima conditions. I have to say though that I witnessed on occasions a rather liberal interpretation of VFR weather minima as practised by some members of the previously mentioned type of flyer.

On the other hand IFR flights operate regardless of weather conditions. It can be a clear blue sky with unlimited visibility and yet airlines in certain areas of semi-controlled airspace (I'll come to that point shortly) invariably select to conduct their flights under IFR. IFR is mandatory of course on the airways system, if for no other reason, than that they wish to enjoy the protection ATC provides. Blackpool's airline being a case in point.

For starters, I will concentrate on our VFR operations, as they constitute most of our workload.

The area where we could effect positive control was limited in size. It being the ATZ whose dimensions I have already stated. Within this area we as controllers were responsible for taxiing, take off, circuit flying, off circuit details, transit aircraft and landing traffic. The object of the exercise was to ensure as far as possible an uninterrupted flow of traffic without individual aircraft becoming entangled with one another. Not always an easy task, particularly when the circuit was choc-a-bloc with aircraft. Having only one frequency, which at times became extremely cluttered, did not help our task. This drawback didn't help pilots either, in that late circuit calls were inevitable due to R/T congestion. This in turn made the controller's job more difficult in trying to sequence his traffic in an orderly manner. It has to be said though that notwithstanding controller's instructions, the responsibility for avoiding other aircraft in the vicinity rested ultimately with the pilots. Even to the extent that if a pilot thought an instruction from ATC, however well meant, could compromise his safety, he was entitled to rectify the situation of his own accord.

A big advantage that the pleasure flying fraternity, be they club, private or kindred spirits, enjoyed at Blackpool was the already mentioned availability of four useable tarmacadam runways. So, no matter which direction the wind was coming from, an into-wind take off and landing was nearly always available. The latter fact was particularly appreciated by student pilots and those part time aviators who could only afford to fly on infrequent occasions. Blackpool also enjoyed an exceptional good weather record. Regarding the number of runways available, an interesting fact, if you think about it, is that pilots had a choice of 'eight' different take-off and landing directions. This was almost unheard of at other airports.

One slight fly in the ointment was, contrary to most standard circuit direction patterns being left hand, our circuit directions were variable, due to the proximity of a contractor's aerodrome, Warton, situated 5 miles east south east, as the crow flies. Our variable circuit's patterns were necessary to avoid conflicting situations with Warton traffic in their own ATZ, particularly as they operated fast jet traffic. As a measure of separating our traffic from Warton's, all our take off's and landings towards the sea were right hand circuits. Those inland, were the standard left hand ones. In other words, the object of the exercise was to aim our traffic away from the boundaries of Warton's ATZ, by picturing the geographical relationship of our respective airports.

Whilst on the subject of circuit direction patterns, it should be borne in mind that the pilot of the aircraft, excepting helicopters, and irrespective of experience status, normally occupies the left hand seat in the cockpit. This, apart from being the normal pilot in command cockpit position, enables him to always keep the active runway in sight, if he/she is on a left-hand circuit. On the other hand, a right hand circuit does not afford the same view of the active runway. Furthermore, if a second pilot, more usually the instructor, is occupying the right hand seat in the cockpit, the pilot in command has an even more restricted view of the runway, on a right hand circuit pattern detail.

Due to these variable traffic patterns, ATC was not always very popular when sudden wind changes necessitated a change in runway which, in turn, invariably meant a change in circuit direction.

A classic example of how such rapid changes of runway direction occurred was brought about by the following weather phenomena, which happened frequently at our airport, particularly during the summer months. This phenomenon was known as the Sea Breeze effect. This meant that the wind started off in an Easterly direction, then as the sun got up and the land mass warmed, the wind would quite rapidly swing round in a clock-wise direction, from East to South, thence Westwards, ending up in a West to Northwest direction. Conversely, at the end of the day, it would unwind back to where it started. No wonder some confusion was generated by this wind factor, obliging pilots to re-orientate themselves in the applicable circuit pattern, almost at a moment's notice.

It was our job in ATC to try and sort this lot out, minimise collision risks and hopefully restore some semblance of order out of apparent chaos! It became even more interesting when schedules, visiting aircraft and others had to be slotted in amongst the circuit activity! During periods of intense activity, our boss had a novel idea. Dispense with normal circuit position calls, they being the 'downwind' and 'finals' position reports, and clear all aircraft to finals. Then, sort it out from there! He even went further. For example, he was of the opinion that any aircraft inbound from the I.O.M. for instance, being our most used inbound route and, assuming we were on a Westerly landing runway, they were, in his mind, already 'downwind' in our circuit, the moment they were airborne from the I.O.M. – all of 70 plus miles away! I was not aware that our circuit extended that far! Not, I suspect, the way ATC was intended to control a circuit pattern. Mind you, there were times when one was tempted to adopt his controlling methods, what with the constant R/T chatter and the number of aircraft milling around the circuit area.

What I have described so far in dealing with VFR activity was good training in mastering the technique of Aerodrome Control, which accounted for most of our time whilst on duty. In fact, in the Ministry days, Blackpool was recognised as one of the best aerodromes, together with the Approach Control function, as a training unit for budding controllers.

So far, I have only dealt with VFR traffic within the ATZ. What about those aircraft that left the circuit area, on local flights or departing elsewhere? Once the latter details were out of our airspace, they were no longer under positive control. Pilots on these details were responsible for their own separation from other aircraft in their vicinity. ATC, in these circumstances, was purely advisory. Not unlike the FIR controller's terms of reference, mentioned in the text about Barton Hall. Now that I have described what I call the 'bread and butter' part of why ATC exists in the first place, let me now turn your attention to what I term the 'meat' of our profession, that being the all important separation of IFR traffic. Without getting too technical, I shall try to explain how we controlled such activity, bearing in mind that our airport was 'outside' the airways system and consequently our area of positive control was rather limited.

The resident airline operating the I.O.M. and Belfast route was not unlike a conveyor belt of continuous aircraft movements, the frequency of which, certainly during the summer months, amounted to a daily total of 36 schedules each way and we were not even open 24 hours a day. Being passenger carrying aircraft, our airline sought the protection of ATC on this busy route and therefore, regardless of the weather, they invariably filed IFR flight plans. These plans activated those ATC agencies responsible for separating aircraft. In our case these were Preston Airways, Ronaldsway (The I.O.M. airport) and ourselves. Separation of such traffic was, as stated, by procedural methods. The criteria, in these instructions, was governed by what is known as 'separation standards minima', as detailed in the Manual of Air Traffic Control.

It is important to bear in mind that the era I am referring to was before Radar covered our area of operations. Consequently, separation of aircraft by procedural means, was the only way ATC could prevent aircraft becoming entangled with one an other. Yet another reason for having an ATC service.

As a perfect example of what I am trying to convey to the reader is the following scenario. The I.O.M. is approximately 70nm West North West of Blackpool. The route between the two airports is served by what is known as an Advisory Route (ADR). This kind of partial controlled airspace has its limitations, in as much that aircraft wishing to participate in this kind of airspace, are known to the ATC authorities, by virtue of their filed flight plans. Therefore they are only separated from other known traffic flying the same route. As indicated, there are certain drawbacks to ADRs as aircraft flying along them do not enjoy full ATC protection, but at least it does provide some measure of control, better than none at all.

I do not propose to go into all the examples of how we utilised all the different procedural separation criteria at our disposal, but for obvious reasons, height spacing was near the top of the list. All I will say is that with the type of limited airspace we had, in which to exercise positive control, we could, if necessary, apply all the different separation methods laid down. A further spacing element was that, all aircraft taking part in the ADR service, were subject to what is known as the Quadrantal rule. This means aircraft flew specific heights relative to the track they would be using. In our scenario then, aircraft bound for Ronaldsway flew at say 4500 or 6500 feet. Conversely, aircraft inbound from Ronaldsway were 1000 feet lower, standard vertical separation, say 3500 or 5500 feet. Also, to make the picture that much clearer, the aircraft's (at this stage they were mainly Dakotas) elapsed time between the two airports, was in the region of 25-30 minutes, depending upon the wind direction and strength.

Now we come to the interesting part of this separation exercise. Due to the en-route vertical spacing required by ATC, it meant that opposite direction aircraft had to be 1000 feet apart from10 minutes before until 10 minutes after they are deemed to have passed each other en-route. In practical terms, due to the type of aircraft flying this route and, bearing in mind their elapsed times, once such aircraft were simultaneously airborne from both airports – a not uncommon occurrence – they almost immediately found themselves in a conflicting separation situation. Maybe hard to believe but it was a fact. Now, our job as controllers, unless the en-route controlling authority Preston airways had issued specific instructions to the contrary, was to 'juggle' our aircraft around in such a manner as to resolve this particular separation conundrum. As we, at Blackpool, operated the higher level aircraft, illustrated earlier, it fell upon us to achieve the required vertical separation. The only way we could do this was to instruct our departing aircraft, to climb overhead or, stay, to the North and East, in other words away from their eventual en-route flight path, until the said aircraft had passed the height of the opposing traffic. Only then could we allow our aircraft to set course for its destination. Such delays, before aircraft could set course, didn't always go down very well with some passengers, such as businessmen having to keep timed appointments, not to mention the extra workload imposed upon pilots carrying out such gymnastics but, I repeat, it was the only way we could ensure safe operations on this busy route.

There was, however, one method we could employ to avoid such delays, that being the weather conditions on route. If conditions were such that aircraft, despite electing to operate under IFR, could climb or descend visually, known in the trade as complying with visual meteorological conditions (VMC). Then aircraft could be instructed to carry out such manoeuvres direct on course, thus obviating the necessity of having to 'juggle' them around, to achieve the desired result. Provided, of course, the pilots concerned, accepted such instructions and were made aware of the opposite direction traffic situation. This visual 'let-out', I must admit, saved a lot of 'aggro' on behalf of pilots and controllers alike.

I know I have dwelt on this aspect of ATCs input at such length, nevertheless, we controllers were confronted with these situations quite frequently. Now it can be seen why such emphasis was placed on knowing one's separation standards like the back of your hand, which was instilled into us from the beginning of our ATC careers. Throughout my own involvement in this profession, I never lost sight of the importance attached to these rulings. Even when radar became a widespread facility, there was always the danger that someone would inadvertently pull the plug on the radar display, which meant a rapid return to procedural separation.

Incidentally, having mentioned radar, it would be remiss of me not to explain why this facility, to a large extent, reduced the delays inherent in procedural separation. Let me give you an example.

Take two identical types of aircraft flying the same route and at the same height. Under procedural control these aircraft would have to be spaced 10 minutes apart which is equivalent, in distance of approximately 30nm. Under radar control, this distance can be reduced to 5nm. Furthermore, the radar separation applies no matter what the attitude of an aircraft in relation to another, be they climbing, descending, banking or whatever. Small wonder then that radar control has largely replaced the former procedural element of ATC's operations.

That just about sums up what my colleagues, and I was faced with in the early days or our employment at Blackpool Airport.

Our controlling skills can be summarised as concentrating on sequencing VFR traffic within the circuit area, ensuring IFR traffic got the protection from other users of our airspace and, last but by no means least, integrating all this activity in the interests of ATC's motto, 'maintaining a safe, orderly and expeditious flow of traffic'. Easier said than done. Time would tell whether we were up to it.

Now for the next challenge I was faced with, taking up the reigns of a SATCO post. Before I relate my experiences as the boss, one final word as to what, if anything had transpired to date. Ironically I cannot recall anything of note, or unusual occurrences, that happened during this initial three-year period. All I can say, on reflection, is that it enabled me to gain invaluable operational experience and at the same time settle into my chosen venue of employment.

As it happened, the more interesting events, occurrences, etc. seemed to materialise after I had become SATCO. Maybe this was due to some of the characters, diverse in nature, with their own idiosyncrasies, who worked for and with me, during my term in the office.

The following pages will, I hope, enliven the narrative and show the reader that despite the serious nature of our profession, there was a humorous side to our activities.

Promotion to SATCO – 1965-1981

In three short years I had gained invaluable experience which I hoped, would stand me in good stead in my up and coming elevation to SATCO status.

1965 was to prove significant on two counts. First, my promotion to the number one position that could be achieved in a local government run airport ATC set-up and second, the introduction of a talk-down radar. A welcome addition to our limited radio navigation aids.

Presumably I had kept my nose clean in the eyes of the powers to be as a consequence of which, in just eight years in ATC, I had reached the pinnacle of my vocation in life. What follows are my philosophies, reminiscences, anecdotes, etc that spanned the sixteen years I spent in the 'hot seat'. They are not necessarily in sequence, being no diarist. Rather they are an overall picture of the type of life I experienced during my term in office. I am also taking the opportunity, later on, of describing some of the interesting characters that worked for me, without whom, my story would be lifeless.

On setting foot in my office, complete with its occupants title displayed on the door, one of the first tasks I undertook was to peruse the extensive filing system I had inherited from my predecessor. There and then I decided there were far too many files, the contents of which, after a perfunctory look through, I decimated to half their original size. Consequently, I spent the rest of my time in office, looking for correspondence that I had consigned to the WPB! I have always been an impulsive person. The previous occupant was known to be a past master at generating bumf, a fact of life that I was 'not' noted for. I like to think I was, by nature, more orientated towards the practical things of life. I do accept that some paper work is inevitable in any walk of life, but I admit, this was one of my lesser attributes as an administrator.

How then, one might ask, did I visualise my role in my newfound status? My priorities, as I saw them were, to a certain extent, dictated by the unavoidable ATC staffing levels that I knew I would be faced with. This in actual fact, played right into my hands as I had already decided, rightly or wrongly, that I had no intention of being purely an administrative type of SATCO. I wished to remain, first and foremost, an operational controller, preferably leading from the front. As indicated earlier, I really had no choice in the matter as it happened.

Although I did not appear as a permanent fixture on the controllers watch roster, I might just as well have done. I had to provide sickness relief and cover those lengthy periods when new controllers, having replaced those that had elected to leave our employ, had to undergo a minimum 'in house' period of training, known in the profession as Minimum Experience Required (MER) before they could operate solo. Furthermore, not only did I wish to lead a team of professionals by, hopefully setting an example for others to follow but, also, try and master all aspects of ATC operations. A task that I knew would take time to achieve. No doubt I am stating the obvious in how I intended to operate, seeing I was supposed to be the top dog!

As a result of my self proclaimed order of priorities, my office duties tended to be relegated, like my filing system, to a backwater number. As it happened, I was fortunate that my administrative duties did not command much of my time and in any case, by appointing Pete as my deputy, he was willing to assist me in any problems that arose. Furthermore, he undertook a chore that I had never been involved in. That being the all-important task of preparing controller watch rosters, something that he displayed an aptitude for. In the long run I did manage to master this particular technique.

Another essential part of my responsibilities was to ensure that all my staff were conversant with the latest procedures, regulations, etc. that regularly infiltrate our profession. So as not to be accused of deliberately withholding vital information, I devised a system whereby each member of staff, initialled a pro-forma, as an indication that they had read and understood, whatever missive had been brought to their attention. No doubt other SATCOs adopted similar measures. My assistants were given the unenviable task of keeping our library of documents current with the never-ending stream of amendments. Other tasks that were considered necessary for the smooth running of the unit, I also tended to delegate. Is it not said that the 'art of good management is delegation'? I subscribed to that view and, acted accordingly. Some would say I over did it! On the other hand, I would never ask any members of my staff to undertake a task that I was not prepared to do myself. Being, to all intents and purposes, a watch-keeping SATCO, enabled me to put into practice those aspects of ATC I felt strongly about.

One of the admitted drawbacks of my semi permanent involvement in the controlling scene was that I tended to wear my ATC hat to the exclusion of my other responsibilities, namely in respect of my superiors. They considered that a SATCO should be involved in the higher echelons of management. Not surprisingly then my popularity stakes in that quarter, were not always what they should have been! Nevertheless I was content to settle in my role as the Senior Controller and conduct ATC operations in such a manner that, ultimately I hoped, would benefit us all. By that I am implying that my favourite hobbyhorse of fostering a good ATC/Pilot relationship was my main aim.

I was aware that in some ATC units, appreciation of each others operational conduct was not always apparent and not helped by ATC's image in some quarters. For example, some of our 'customers' looked upon ATC at airports as 'gods in their Ivory towers' who considered their word as law.

That kind of attitude bothered me. One way or another, I was determined throughout my career as the SATCO, and beyond, when I reverted to being an ordinary controller, that I would try and dispel this image which we had been lumbered with. That's why the theme throughout my memoirs hinges on the various ways I adopted to counteract this state of affairs.

What I wanted to achieve was a spirit of co-operation, a community spirit if you like, between the parties on both sides of the ATC/Pilots divide. In relation to the resident airline pilots, I was off to a good start as I had flown with a number of them prior to my entry into ATC. Such people as 'Johnnie' Johnson, the Chief Pilot, Eric Skemp, Alec Watson, Lech and others, whose names I cannot recall, with whom I enjoyed a good relationship, both professionally and personally. If I could enlist the support of the resident flying clubs, their instructors, their students, and private pilots, by preaching my philosophy, I was firmly of the opinion that, in the long term, we could all derive mutual benefit. I felt this theory of mine could be particularly applicable to an airport's operations, such as ours, where, due to the nature of the 'mix' of traffic involved, it could be described as a 'general aviation' type of aerodrome. I did realise however that what I was trying to achieve would not necessarily apply to other ATC units, such as those operating at major commercial airports, airways centres, control zones, and similar establishments.

I also considered the two alternatives whereby ATC could project their image. Firstly they could adopt a dogmatic and dictatorial approach to controlling aircraft or, secondly, the method I preferred of, applying the rules of the game without fear or favour and certainly without rancour. In a nutshell, I was a firm believer in both 'sides of the fence' working together, without being at loggerheads with each other. Not that I am implying this was the situation prior to my involvement in Blackpool's ATC set-up. As an added comment, I suppose we were, after all, custodians of all who flew in our skies but NOT in the way some would portray our role.

There was one avenue of concern, right on our doorstep which, hopefully will illustrate my attitude towards the private sector of operations, mainly among the Flying club fraternity. For instance, they tended to carve up one another within the circuit area and generally behave in an anti-social manner. No doubt this was partly caused by inter club rivalry which was an unwelcome trait in their activities. To try and alleviate this problem it seemed to me that what was really required, to regularise this state of affairs, was a civil version of what is standard practise in the R.A.F., i.e. a Wing Commander flying. Not being a military aerodrome, I knew that such a draconian measure would not be tolerated by our civilian flyers. Instead, I proposed a get together of all the club CFI's, their instructors, plus a representative of the private pilots, no mean feat in itself, so I was subsequently told! My idea was to meet around a table to discuss ways and means of improving circuit discipline and responsible airmanship, thereby avoiding the necessity of ATC having to lay down rigid rules and regulations. By merely being able to convene this meeting with full attendance of the parties concerned, I submit, was an example of the steadily increasing rapport that was being established.

The end result of this meeting, knowing full well that I would be unable to appoint a singular person to undertake the role I originally envisaged, was a document drawn up by myself entitled 'locally agreed procedures.' These encompassed such avenues as height, spacing within and adjacent to the circuit area, asking pilots to vary their speeds whilst carrying out circuit and bump details to avoid bunching up. Additionally delaying tactics if the circuit was fully occupied, by holding off aircraft, at selected geographical points situated within a five mile radius of the airport. In other words, create a buffer zone between circuit and off-circuit activity. In actual fact the latter idea was put into official practice later on in my career, and the selected holding areas were entitled Visual Reporting Points (VRPs).

All these matters, and others, were mutually agreed at this meeting with the emphasis on the word 'agreed'. The object of the exercise was that both ATC and the clubs would abide by the written word. All this, of course, was in the name of improving operating standards and ensuring, as far as humanly possible, a safe flying environment.

I was pleasantly surprised at the reactions to my proposal and, when implemented, the procedures worked like a charm, at least for a while! Inevitably, as club instructors departed elsewhere, being replaced by others, a never ending scene in the instructional world, the message was not always passed on. Hence refresher meetings had to be held at regular intervals to keep the agreed procedures current.

This scheme of mine must have impressed my successors as the original document, with the odd amendment, is still incorporated in local ATC orders 33 years after I introduced it. I like to think this was one of my more successful contributions as the SATCO.

Another barrier I wished to break down was the reluctance pilots felt, except those on business, of paying us a visit to see how we operated, and list any problems they may wish to discuss. If nothing else, I hoped it would indicate to them that we were, after all, from the same species of the human race, not robots governed solely by rules and regulations.

On a social level, all the flying clubs were 'open house' to us. There were some parties of note that we attended! Even the airline 'boys' were not averse to socialising with us; they too threw some memorable 'do's'. All good stuff in the interests of harmonious relationships.

Now for some personnel recollections to inject a bit of humour into the proceedings.

I, despite my status, was not immune to some of the antics our pilot colleagues and we got up to.

Yours truly even achieved brief TV fame! I was 'persuaded' to take part in an episode of the then well known children's programme 'Sooty'. This particular episode centred on the airport. My role was somewhat short lived, in that all I was required to do was clear Sooty for take-off. This was filmed in the control tower with me talking to a puppet! I don't think somehow I was cut out for this sort of thing. My old flying pal, Hoaggy, my best man at my wedding in 1954, couldn't believe his eyes when he saw me one afternoon on the goggle box, whilst idly watching TV at his home, in far off Devon. He rang me to ask me if he wasn't seeing things!

No prizes for guessing what my new title became! Initially, I do not recall Sooty being cleared to land so, maybe he's still airborne.

On another occasion, one of my assistants, Barbara, who, if memory serves me right, was the first female member of our ATC unit since the Ministry days, reminded me of the day when I arrived at work one morning, still wearing my pyjamas under my normal attire. I think it must have been one of those times where I had imbibed rather too well the night before at some party or other. Apart from being improperly dressed, I was still clearing a scheduled flight for take-off, bound for the I.O.M. when, in fact, the aircraft was already half way there! Fortunately the pilot, Bryan Armstrong, knew me better than to normally behave in such an irrational manner, and promptly dismissed my indiscretion as a one-off lapse in professional standards. Not, I suppose the kind of example a SATCO should set. However, my reputation appeared to be none the worse, for all that. Proof that humanity, whatever the circumstances, is capable of the odd lapse in professional standards.

The following example of our ATC/Pilot rapport is quite amusing. Pete became inadvertently 'tied up' with a couple of our airline skippers. To put it bluntly, they were as queer as hell and, because of Pete's relatively handsome features, they took a shine to him. For instance, every time he was on duty and these characters were flying a scheduled service, whilst they were on their take-off run, charging down the runway, a hand would appear out of the cockpit window accompanied by the following exchange over the R/T. "I'm waving to you Pete", repeated several times! What other pilots, listening out on the frequency, thought of this verbal exchange, I can only leave to one's imagination. Not surprisingly, Pete took some time to live this one down. To set the record straight, he was NOT that way inclined. He had a wife and four kids to prove he was normal. There are more anecdotes to come shortly just to prove that we professionals do have our lighter moments.

With reference to the club and private sector of our workload, whenever we tended to get bogged down with the amount of traffic we had to cope with, really the fault in such situations was largely of our own doing. In some cases it was a question of one-upmanship. Who could outdo the other in handling as many aircraft as possible! No doubt a certain amount of favouritism, with club personnel, entered into the equation. A case of making rods for our own backs which, if we weren't careful, could get out of hand. Popularity does not always work to one's advantage. Situations whereby 'the best laid plans of mice and men' could be a very apt description of the pitfalls we could let ourselves in for.

To ease our workload during periods of intense activity, expedition was the name of the game. Here our task was made easier by having four runways to choose from.

To avoid long queues of aircraft waiting to take-off, invariably we used one runway for departures, and another for landings. The only problem here was when we had to use the westerly runways i.e. the main and the subsidiary one, where their upwind ends converged. In these situations, one had to ensure that departing traffic would be airborne well before they had reached the upwind end of the runway and, at the same time, instruct landing traffic NOT to land long on the other runway. Otherwise there may have been expensive noises where the runways met – a controlling situation that tended to be frowned upon by our regulating authority, the CAA inspectorate. In my experience though, their fears were unfounded. If one used the same two runways, when the wind was from the East, their alignment diverged, thereby enabling controllers to expedite their traffic even more quickly than the Western runway configuration – a good example of using one's resources to the advantage of the pilots and ourselves.

In fact, one of my controllers, Vic Jackson, known to all as 'Jacko', took this method of control a stage further. Being an ex-wartime pilot used to take-off's and landings regardless of the wind factor, he believed that anyone who flew aeroplanes, regardless of their experience or, more often, lack of it, could cope with the wind factor whichever direction it was blowing from. He was a great believer in keeping the traffic flowing, numbers did not bother him, so, his idea of expedition was to depart and land aircraft utilising every available bit of concrete. He used any number of directions, preferably nearest to the control tower, in his way of thinking, his methods saved taxiing time. Whenever he was controlling, Blackpool took on the appearance of a mini Chicago O'Hare. Economy in all things was his byword as witness the fact that his instructions to pilots were often delivered in monosyllables, never using two words when one would do. All very expeditious remembering ATCs motto, but not always appreciated by inexperienced and student pilots. Incidentally, his idea of the equipment required in a control tower was very basic. He was of the opinion that all that was required was two trestle tables, a transmit and receive system, and two Aldis lamps!

As an indication of the more eccentric part of this personality, the following gems I think are worth recalling. Before relating his culinary delights I ought to point out that at this stage, our working environment had no separate dining facilities, even the kitchen was too small. As a consequence, all our re-fuelling needs had to be accommodated whilst on duty in the control tower. Proper meal breaks, at this stage of our careers, were not countenanced. Anyway, back to Jacko. He had a penchant for enormous fry-ups, the ingredients of which left a lot to be desired. For example, out of date sprouts, bacon with a distinct blue tinge, old cheese, stale bread etc, all of which was carefully sought out from the local shop, at reduced prices. This 'mess' was fried up together in a frying pan that had seen better days and devoured with gusto. His constitution must have been cast iron. A further eccentricity, worth recording, was the way he dressed for work, particularly during the winter months. We reckon his wardrobe came mostly from the local Oxfam shop. He could often be seen wandering around the airfield wearing a tea cosy on his head, on which the holes for the spout and handle acted, presumably as ventilation. What a character, the likes of which made my life in ATC interesting. Not long after he joined me I discovered he was on the Berlin Airlift based at the same place as I was. He was still in the R.A.F. me being a civilian flyer, our paths never crossed.

By contrast, two of my controllers, known as the two Ron's contrived one way or another to limit club activity, which was anathema to them. Not a very popular move with the clubs as they, quite rightly, wanted their aircraft to be utilised fully. Mind you, they unashamedly socialised with those very persons whose activities they tried to curtail. If the truth be known, these two gentlemen's idea of an ATC service was that it should be confined to commercial operations only, quite forgetting that the club flying was a form of commercialism anyway. 'Tiddlers', as they irreverently called them, should in their opinion be banished to disused wartime airfields dotted around the countryside, having no need for ATC. Another of their ploys whenever they were on duty was that, on the slightest pretext, particularly if it looked as though the traffic situation was building up, they would either resort to pro-longed telephone calls or carry out a so called airfield inspection, leaving whoever was on duty with them to cope on their own. Their standard R/T instructions when they became harassed was' you fly your aircraft boy, I'll do the Air Traffic control '; this was Ron Reilly's favourite comment. The other Ron, Stewarts's pet utterances were 'ring the tower when you land'; 'you're not doing that on my licence'; 'negative' or 'overshoot', I say again overshoot'.

Ron Stewart was a Scotsman and Ron Reilly was an Anglo-Indian. Both were small in stature which may have accounted for the reason that they appeared to get on together like a house on fire. They invariably argued the toss amongst themselves and occasionally give me a headache into the bargain, sorting out their nefarious activities. Despite my criticism, they were friendly types as typified by the following comments. Ron Stewart tried to introduce me to the world of golf even persuading me to become a member of his club. I regret I did not live up to his expectations. I was a complete amateur by comparison. I enjoy the game and still play it to this day although my handicap was, and still is, the game itself!

Ron Reilly shared my interest in Jazz music. When sober, he was quite an accomplished clarinet player and being coloured, singing wise, he could mimic Louis Armstrong to a tee. On one occasion however, he blotted his copybook. A party was being held in one of the clubs at which the well-known trumpet player Nat Gonella was performing. Ron had previously expressed a desire to play with Nat but for his sins, he got so pissed he couldn't play a note! He too, like Jacko, had a penchant for so called culinary delights in that, when the mood took him, he would conjure up enormous curries in the tower kitchen, stinking the whole building out.

Bearing in mind his colour, he used to amuse me on hot summer days, when I used to ask him what he was going to do on his days off. Without batting an eyelid he would say, "I think I'll go down to the beach and do a spot of sun bathing."

Eventually these two characters left our employ and departed to much quieter pastures, more in keeping with their idea of ATC. Their chosen aerodromes were in the Outer Hebrides and Lands End; no prizes for guessing who went where! Having given a light-hearted account of some of the characters who made life in ATC a somewhat amusing experience, I will now, for the time being, revert to reality.

A large part of our activities centred round student pilots as a result of which, we considered it our duty to pay more attention to their activities as compared to the more experienced types. We also recognised that student pilots naturally concentrated more on flying their machines; therefore we tended to keep our instructions to them to a minimum. Of course we had our part to play in the scheme of things but due to the R/T congestion problem and their understandable reluctance to use the radio, they didn't always comply with our instructions immediately they were issued. The problem was that a lot of these gentlemen were, quite frankly, frightened to death of using their radio, in the first instance. They seemed to 'freeze' when they had to communicate with ATC, occasions where we had to bite our tongues and exercise restraint! In other words, adopt the time honoured phrase 'patience is a virtue'. It seemed a better way of overcoming this problem, rather than let things degenerate into a shouting match, which solves nothing. We even devised a scheme that would draw our attention to pilots experience factor. The FPSs denoting a flying detail was annotated with the pilot's name, most of whom were known to us anyway and they likewise knew us from work and social contacts. The more inexperienced ones had the additional letters ES (early students) alongside their names. On instructional details, the instructor's name was the norm. Again we knew most of them, and they knew us individually. There was no doubt in my mind that this idea of identifying the various levels of pilot's capabilities helped us considerably in our controlling duties. Likewise, pilots could feel at ease, in that we were aware of the level of their experience.

Being a busy airport, traffic wise, those who transited in the vicinity of our airspace were only too aware of what was going on and therefore in their own interests, they invariably called us on R/T for traffic information. Such was the level of activity at times, all we could truthfully say to them was the following – 'random VFR traffic, positions and heights unknown' – which brings me conveniently to an annual event that occurs in America.

I wonder if anyone has ever listened, as I have, to a tape recording of controllers trying to sort out those aircraft attending the well known American EAA Convention fly-in at Oshkosh. Their volume of traffic was not dissimilar to what we sometimes had to cope with although, never in a month of Sundays, could we compare their movement rate with ours. They had a novel idea in their R/T method of controlling. They didn't use aircraft call-signs, instead they used aircraft colour schemes to identify traffic, as follows: – "Follow the red and white Cessna ahead; land on the numbers; land left after the blue twin ahead", and so on. An interesting R/T exchange, and a tape worth listening to. To sum up to date, what we had been involved in, and would continue to do, would be the pattern our livelihood in the airports involvement in the aviation scene.

I think I should point out that the views I have expressed, on the way I sought to conduct ATC, are not necessarily shared by my compatriots. All I will say that, no doubt my attitude towards flyers is coloured by my previous involvement in the flying game. I had no intention of losing my affinity with them. I seem to have made this statement previously: my apologies for repeating my sentiments. To complete the picture of the variable activities that confronted us, a word or two about other types of airspace restrictions occasionally imposed upon us is worth noting.

For example, when members of the Royal Family flew into our airport and, dependent upon their status within the royal household some of them enjoyed the protection of what is known as 'purple' controlled airspace, which effectively bars any form of flying, apart from airways and control zone traffic, within the flight path of the Royal aircraft. Incidentally, I have often wondered whether this colour has any significance with Royal attire, or am I confusing the issue with ermine trimmed robes? Both the colour and fabric mentioned, conjure up in my eyes, Royalty and Nobility. Of interest, whenever HRH Prince Philip was piloting the aircraft, he used the R/T call sign 'rainbow'. Whether it was himself who acknowledged my or my colleagues instructions, or he was just monitoring the radio whilst his co-pilot did the talking, we had no way of telling. Nothing like being in a position of controlling the highest in the land!

The other airspace restriction we had to contend with, albeit it was only on rare occasions was when an Air Display was held at our airport. As a matter of interest I, at a later date, was personally involved in organising such an event, the story of which I intend to include in my memoirs later, by way of a contrast to our day to day way of earning our keep.

Even the world renowned R.A.F. Aerobatics Team, the 'Red Arrows' commanded their own protected airspace, whenever they performed at, or in the vicinity, of the airport. For obvious reasons they did not wish to get mixed up with other aircraft that may be flying about. Their airspace envelope covered an area of five miles, from their display datum, and up to a height of 5000 feet.

Some people used to say to me, as though I was some sort of demi-god, "So you controlled the Red Arrows did you?" In truth, the only controlling bit we got involved in was the take-off and landing phase of their performance and their arrival and departures to take part in a display. Once they were airborne and clear of our circuit, they used a 'discreet' frequency so, in essence, they controlled themselves.

At a later date in my time at Blackpool, this team became a regular feature in our calendar of unusual events, in that they nearly always provided a 'grand finale' in our towns annual summer R.A.F. recruiting drive. I, for one, never tired of their displays and always looked forward to the next year's performance.

Talking of unusual events a couple of rare aircraft made their last flights into Blackpool and, if memory serves me right, I was on duty on both occasions.

The first arrival was a full-blown Lancaster bomber that had been flown all the way from Australia to the U.K. and, as luck would have it, its last flight in this country was from somewhere down south to us. Incidentally the pilot was none other than the well-known British Aerobatics champion and R.A.F. test pilot, Neil Williams. To yours truly this was a memorable re-acquaintance with the one aircraft in the R.A.F. that I had fond memories of, as witness my earlier remarks about the Lanc. Of interest, a history of this particular aircraft appears in a booklet entitled 'Story of a Lanc' written and compiled by Brian Goulding and Mike Garbett, the noted authors of Publisher Ian Allan's 'Lancaster at War' series.

Although I didn't know it at the time I was destined to be its guardian during its latter incarceration at our airport. My involvement came about as follows.

Initially this aircraft became the centrepiece static exhibit of a recently formed aviation museum on the airport. Unfortunately, this welcome addition to the airport's image was short lived. Upon the demise of the museum, all the exhibits had to be sold to offset the museum losses.

A local titled gentleman, one Lord Lilford, bought the Lanc. It was at this stage of history where I come into the picture. The aircraft had to be removed from the now defunct museum site parked adjacent the Airport Fire hangar. It so happened that this hangar was situated directly opposite my back garden wall and, the Lanc, so positioned, that I could feast my eyes upon it to my hearts content. Added to which the new owner, having heard of my interest and limited involvement in Lancaster's, appointed me its guardian whilst it languished on its parking spot, awaiting a decision as to its ultimate future. The only drawback being the fact that the aircraft would be wide open to elements. Sure enough, in the course of time, it did become rather dilapidated even to the extent of birds nesting in the cockpit! On the other hand I was given a free hand in looking after this machine, even on occasions, entering its interior (I had the keys to the crew entrance door) and sitting in my old crew position. It reminded me of the days gone by; pure nostalgia I know!

I don't know what exactly went on behind the scenes but RAF Scampton, the well known ex-Dambusters base, in conjunction with his Lordship, decided that this aircraft would be an ideal candidate as Scampton's gate guardian as a reminder of its association with Scampton's history.

As a result of this decision, a team of technicians came from Scampton and spent a couple of weeks or so dismantling the Lanc: and transporting it, bit by bit, back to the Lincolnshire aerodrome.

In due course, entirely in their spare time, they restored the aircraft, both internally and externally to its original pristine condition. Just as though it had come straight off the manufacturers assembly line.

When the time came to display it as intended, I'm told it was quite a juggling act to manoeuvre it into position, due to the number of buildings in the vicinity of Scampton's main gate.

Because of my involvement I was invited to the official unveiling ceremony, followed by a reception in the Officers Mess.

When I saw the Lanc I could not believe my eyes, the 'boys' at Scampton had done a remarkable job in restoring the old war-horse.

The way I attended the ceremony could I suppose, have a sense of irony about it. I motored down in my recently acquired brand new Mercedes car. Whereas the Lanc was my all time favourite aircraft, the Merc I held in similar esteem, as being the one motoring marque it had been my ambition to own.

Whether the combination of a wholly designed and manufactured British masterpiece, and an ex enemy product, albeit the latter was a different mode of transport, went hand in glove, I don't know. All I can say is that at the material time they were my contrasting sentiments. Nevertheless a memorable occasion which I was proud to play a small part in.

The second rarity to appear on the scene was a Vulcan bomber. An impressive aircraft both in size and the noise it generated.

It was bought by one of the local flying club owners for the princely sum of £5000! And to think they cost millions when new; what a bargain.

I have an idea this aircraft took part in the Falklands conflict but, I may be mistaken.

Like the Lanc it never flew again. Its final resting-place was beside this particular clubhouse building, over which the starboard wing stands as a sentinel. The club owner charges a nominal fee to the general public who wish to look inside the aircraft, thereby earning its keep.

The Vulcan is still there to this day and can be readily seen as one enters Blackpool Airport's main entrance.

The Introduction of Radar – 1965

This was, in my mind, the second most important thing, that just happened to coincide with my promotion. One must get one's priorities right, in order of merit!

The airport authority had decided to invest in a talk-down radar known as the Decca 424. It had its limitations in that it was low powered and, strictly speaking, a one aircraft at a time, landing aid. Originally it was a marine radar adapted for civil aviation use. Being a controller interpreted facility; its usage was entirely dependent on the operator's expertise in its performance. One of its drawbacks was the response of an aircraft's return, as displayed on the radar scope. Due to its low power and wavelength, the 'target' (aircraft) on the radar screen appeared as a pin-prick of light. Modern day radars are considerably more powerful and have a greater wavelength, which increases an aircraft's return on the radar screen as a sizeable blip, which is much more discernible to the operator's eye.

Its worst fault was the effect rain had on the display screen, heavy rain in particular. This kind of weather covered the screen with a mass of pin-pricks, which were indistinguishable from an aircraft response. If you were not careful, you could find yourself controlling a raindrop instead of an aircraft! I nearly fell into this trap on more than one occasion.

On the positive side, foggy conditions were ideal in which to talk an aircraft down. Officially, one could conduct a talk-down to within 200 ft and half a mile from the runway's end. Not infrequently though, if conditions were that bad and one 'chose' to ignore the official line, talk-downs were continued until the aircraft was about to land, no problem.

Once the equipment had been installed, and checked out operationally, we discovered that, apart from Pete who had operated similar equipment at his previous place of employment, there was no one qualified to use it! However, all was not lost as the rest of the controllers, including myself, had radar ratings in our licences, therefore all that was required was a period of MER before we could offer it operationally. In my case, you will recall that I had done a radar course whilst at Barton Hall which, at the time, I thought was a wasted effort but now became a bonus in my aerodrome ATC career.

I can well remember my first solo talk-down in 'anger'. It was a typical November evening, foggy but just within landing limits. I don't mind admitting that I was a bit apprehensive, as I was entirely on my own; no one to assist me if I got it wrong.

The aircraft concerned was a Constellation, which, incidentally, was one of the largest aircraft to land at Blackpool at that time. Ironically it was piloted by one of my old skippers who, after successfully bringing him in, commented favourably upon my performance. This unsolicited remark did wonders for my confidence. Even if I say it myself, there would be more than one occasion when I would be rewarded by similar remarks from 'satisfied' customers. In my opinion, this aspect of ATC, together with procedural control, was the most rewarding part of the many tasks we had to deal with.

On one occasion though, I did rather blot my copy-book, although there was no risk involved. What I did was to vector (steer) a twin-engined jet around what I thought was a slow moving aircraft – this happened over the Irish Sea to the west of Blackpool, only to discover on completion of the manoeuvre, I had taken avoiding action on a fast moving ship! An embarrassing episode which I was not allowed to forget, for a time anyway!

Our new piece of technology also proved to be a lifesaver as witness the following couple of episodes. Pete was the radar controller on both occasions and the incidents I am about to relate, involved a certain type of pilot I have previously described. None other than the so-called instant 'ace of the base', although he had recently qualified as a PPL. His name was McCabe, appropriately nick-named 'Killer McCabe'. I can do no better than quote Pete's words as to what happened. On the first occasion, "this pilot took off from Rufforth to Blackpool, against all advice, on his first solo cross country flight as a PPL and I had to talk him down to the end of the runway, in a cloud base of 300ft". "Another time he took off from Belfast at night, lost his instruments over the sea opposite Thornton whereby I stopped him from crashing when, by using the radar, I was able to tell him he was in a spiral dive to the right in cloud".

The advantage of having this facility compared to the less precise aids we already had, enabled many more successful landings to be made than hitherto had been the case. It was a costly piece of equipment which more than paid for its upkeep for some time to come.

By the time it had passed its 'sell by date', to use a modern expression, I had carried out an approximate number of 2500 talk-downs for real, plus many others as practise and familiarisation exercises.

6   ROTARY AIR PAGEANT

What follows became a total surprise, and a real feather in my cap, due entirely to my professional standing.

A business friend of mine, a Rotarian, who happened to be a private pilot, by the name of John Halliwell, invited me to become a member of the Rotary movement. For those not familiar with this charitable organisation, it is an international body of professional men, from all walks of life who, amongst other things, do sterling work on projects to help the community. This body is divided into clubs, which are to be found in practically every town and city throughout the land. Similar clubs exist in other countries worldwide. It originated in America and such is its membership, in this country, that I can only liken it to Freemasonry. Unlike the latter though, there is no mystique about its activities.

One cannot volunteer. You have to be proposed and seconded by Rotarians and, provided your credentials are up to specification, you are duly inducted as a Rotarian. As I hadn't a clue as to what Rotary was all about, until enlightened, I felt honoured that I was considered a suitable candidate for such an august body of men. Upon being accepted, amongst other things, I was presented with my Rotary Lapel Badge, which I unashamedly wore with pride.

Regrettably, after five year as a Rotarian, I had no alternative but to terminate my membership. The problem was the weekly luncheon meeting, being one of the requirements of membership. Being a shift worker I could only attend these luncheons when I was on a day off which meant I was snookered from going out for the day with my family. Evening meetings would have been, at least for me and I suspect others, a more convenient time of the day for such gatherings. Tradition however dictated otherwise.

Nevertheless, I will always be grateful to my benefactor for introducing me to an organisation that commands worldwide respect.

I like to think I left my mark as a Rotarian in what follows. I, and John, in a moment of madness, seeing I had only been a member a couple of years, suggested as a means of raising funds for charity, organising a Rotary Air Display at our home airport.

What possessed us to open our mouths, I hesitate to say, but our challenge was accepted so no way could we back off now!

It was probably the most ambitious project that any Rotary Club had undertaken. Strictly speaking, my involvement in such a project did not come within my terms of reference as the SATCO. Nevertheless, in a roundabout sort of way, I was putting our airport on the map and, consequently, promoting its suitability as a display venue. I was supported in my endeavours by the Airport Director, Robert Bagshaw, who was quite happy for me to waive my normal duties in disrupting his airport, on behalf of Rotary.

This event took place in October 1969, which, amongst other things, celebrated the 60th anniversary of the First Air Display recognised by the Royal Aero Club, which took place on our aerodrome. Incidentally, in those days it was better known as Squire's Gate aerodrome. Even today some people still refer to it by that name.

Shortly after the event, I wrote a narrative describing all that transpired in the mammoth task we had set ourselves. So, as a break from the more normal route of our day to day activities, I will now insert my 'screed' by way of a contrast to my memoirs.

I actually submitted my MSS to one or two well-known aviation publishers. One in particular, *Aeroplane Monthly*, commented favourably upon my efforts and the way I presented them. Unfortunately they said it was too long for serialisation and too short for a book. I finally got lucky this time around.

The idea

"An Air Display... what a damn good idea!" said John over a pint of beer. What a loosener of the tongue that beverage can be! Little did I realise what I was letting myself in for when I suggested, half jokingly in the bar that night, that an Air Display might be a way of raising funds for charity on behalf of the club. In the final analysis, the venture was a success and raised £3000 in aid of charity.

This story though is about how two amateurs, both by the name of John, set about organising an air Display without the slightest idea of how to go about it. On the road to eventual success there were many pitfalls, frustrations both personal and official, which had I foreseen, I doubt whether I would have been so keen to have opened my 'big mouth' in the first place. However, the dye was cast, so we had no alternative but to prove to ourselves that action could, and would, supersede mere beer talk.

As I have said, a drink can work wonders but, at the same time, it can also get you into a lot of trouble when the tongue happens to slip!

The question might well be asked "why write about a form of public entertainment that occurs on numerous occasions annually throughout the length and breadth of the British Isles?" Be that as it may, they nevertheless never cease to attract the public in large numbers. Furthermore, and I stand to be corrected, I have yet to come across a book or story, apart from advice pamphlets and official memoranda, which records what goes on behind the scenes in organising such an event, hence the reason for this epistle.

Also, I would like to think that this story indicates what a small band of dedicated persons, bearing in mind that this was their first ever venture in organising such a project, can produce in their spare time, providing the enthusiasm is there. One must also remember that an exercise of this magnitude is really a full time occupation and therefore the efforts that were put into our own particular Air Display are truly remarkable. They must serve as a tribute not only to those intimately involved but also to all other club members and outside agencies, who contributed so generously on our behalf.

One other purpose for scribing this narrative, be it for posterity or some similar motive, is the fact that there are other charitable organisations similar to ours who are constantly devising ways and means of 'laying-on' interesting public spectacles which they, in turn, hope will make handsome contributions towards worthwhile charities.

Maybe the contents of this narrative will provide them with food for thought. Who knows, even the professionals of this game may be enlightened by some of the methods we resorted to!

Then and Now – some details of the 1909 meeting we were commemorating

"The next event of importance was the simultaneous promo-tion of the first two flying meetings to be held in this country at

Blackpool and Doncaster respectively. A very great deal of bad feeling manifested itself between the organisers of these rival shows, of which that at Blackpool had the backing of the Aero Club and the municipal authorities. The affair at Doncaster owed its conception to so many and diverse influences, that an application was made to the High Court on the opening morning, for the appointment of a receiver to safeguard the takings!

The field at Blackpool comprised three Voisins in the hands of Rougier, Fournier and Mortimer Singer, a lone Henry Farman (50 Gnome), which was flown alternatively by its designer and Louis Paulham. Two Bleriots in charge of Leblanc and Parkinson. Latham's Antoinette, AV Roe's triplane (10 HP 2-cylinder JAP), three anonymous monoplanes, belonging to Messrs. Saunderson, Creese and Neale, a small Bi-plane in the hands of Senor Fernandez. Thus there were a dozen aircraft assembled, of which five got off the ground during the week. Mr. Roe was the first competitor to attempt to fly, but his 10HP J.A.P. was wholly inadequate for its task, and he wisely retired into his hangar and proceeded with the fitting of the 24 HP motor, which he had recently acquired. When this had been done, he succeeded in making one or two short hops with his triplane.

The meeting was memorable on account of Mr. Hubert Latham's spectacular flight in a high wind. The anemometer recorded a mean speed of 20 mph with frequent gusts up to 38 mph, when the Antoinette took off and completed two laps of the course in just over 10 minutes. The flight marked a new departure in aviation. For the first time a pilot had definitely defied the elements by pitting his skill against a gusty wind. It was a very splendid achievement and marked the foundation of Mr. Hubert Latham's reputation as a bad weather pilot.

Mr. Henry Farman once again annexed most of the premier awards, winning £2400 in the aggregate, as compared with £820 won by Mr. Rougier, £530 won by Mr. Paulhan, and £400 won by Mr. Latham. Mr. Farman's best flight was made early in the week when he covered 47 miles 1,544 yards in 1 hour 32 minutes sixteen and four fifths seconds at an average speed of 32 mph."

From History of British Aviation 1908-1914 by R Dallas Brett

"Modus Operandi"

In the first instance, having let enthusiasm run away with us, approval had to be sought from the responsible body of our club who vetted such projects. No doubt they thought we were completely mad to even suggest such a mammoth task. Additionally we had to obtain approval from the authority responsible for the Airport upon which the display would in due course take place. In the latter case, as I was a Senior Official at the Airport our task was possibly made a little easier. Nevertheless both John and myself had to use our persuasive powers to enlist the Airport Director's support in so much that what we proposed was not necessarily a mad-hat scheme.

After his initial reservation about our ideas (understandable because wherever an Air Display is held, the life of the Airport for that particular day is thrown into complete chaos!) he was won over and promised to put the matter before the Airport authorities for their consideration. Eventually both parties agreed in principle and now we could start the ball rolling. This, like all organised events, took time before official blessing was given so already a number of weeks had elapsed since the germination of the original idea and as yet, no further progress had been made. Originally we had intended holding the event in May, but due to unforeseen circumstances, we had to abandon that date. Consequently I had the brilliant idea (depending on one's point of view!) of selecting a date that coincided with the first aviation meeting to be recognised by the Royal Aero Club. This had in fact been held at our Airport in October 1909. There is even a plaque in the Terminal concourse commemorating the event.

Now I know, most people knowing the vagaries of the British climate at that time of year, would tend to think that we were taking one hell of a risk: I must admit that my thoughts were along similar lines, although I didn't voice my opinion to that effect.

I reasoned that if the flimsy old string bag and fabric flying machines of that era could perform at that time of the year then surely modern aircraft should have no difficulty whatsoever. In actual fact that particular October (1969) was reasonably kind to us and the gamble paid off, although the weather did affect part of the display, as will be seen later in the narrative.

The next important step was to ascertain whether anyone would be prepared to participate. In other words, it was quite obvious that before committing ourselves irrevocably, sufficient participation had somehow or other to be generated if the display was going to be assured of a successful outcome. The yardstick we used was quite simply "Insufficient performers, no display". This I suppose is stating the obvious.

Having arrived at this momentous decision, who were we to contact? It occurred to us that the majority of Air Displays had as their backbone the RAF in either team or individual performances. In addition, the other two services, the RN and the Army, were also invariably represented. Having congratulated ourselves on such brilliant thinking, we once more came to a full stop. We hadn't the slightest idea who to approach to fulfil our grandiose scheme. Nevertheless after numerous enquiries, and after having been advised to use the old maxim, "Always ask for more than you expect", letters were dispatched to the appropriate departments of the three services stating our requirements. Possibly the most important of these was the RAF Participation Committee. This incidentally was the start of correspondence between ourselves and various organisations, and individuals, which was to mount up steadily to six inch-thick set of files, on completion of the sortie.

The initial exploratory work was started almost twelve months before the actual 'do' which, in the long run proved none too soon. Before going into more detail concerning the eventual outcome of our enquiries, it is as well to point out that this participation aspect was but one of many items that had to be considered and eventually organised.

We realised that the ground organisation of such an event, or what I prefer to call the "Domestic arrangements", were going to be of almost equal importance and we were guided by a circular obtained from the then Board of Trade which detailed the requirements organisers were expected to comply with. In other words, our Lords and Masters of the United Kingdom aviation world had a great deal to say as far as our arrangements were concerned: talk about "Big Brother" watching over you! Seriously though, this circular and the B.O.T., did prove to be extremely helpful. The document incidentally was two foolscap sheets of fairly close written type, so it is not surprising when we say that we were initially somewhat overawed by its contents, which did nothing to minimise the task we had set ourselves.

In a later chapter, I shall describe in detail how we managed to comply with all the instructions, mainly by the well tried method of beg, borrow or scrounge wherever the opportunity presented itself. This, if nothing else, would reduce our overheads considerably.

It is perhaps worth mentioning at this stage of our story that our ultimate objective was made a lot easier by the mere fact that amongst the members of our club, we had such personages as the Chief of Police and the Chief Fire Officer. The latter person was also the President of our club at the time. Apart from their professions, they were in a position to use their not inconsiderable influences in the right quarters to obtain the necessary personnel and paraphernalia we were going to need to satisfy our own and the Board of Trade requirements.

We also had the services of a local businessman, with his own printing organization. This was going to prove invaluable as he undertook the task of looking after the advertising, programme printing and sundry other duties connected with enlightening the public at large of our intentions. This was also to prove one of the most important aspects in the eventual success of our venture. I believe that as time drew closer to "D" day, his normal business was in danger of becoming extinct. Come to think of it, I think all of us who were intimately involved, also found ourselves in very similar situations.

Another idea we considered was that due to the uncertainty of our climate, a pure flying display would not necessarily, in itself, attract the public in the numbers we optimistically hoped for. We had in mind a figure of 50,000 or so, but with an equally interesting static (ground) display, we would kill two birds with one stone and safeguard against part, or all, of the flying exhibits being cancelled due to weather. This did prove a very worthwhile aspect of our display, No doubt our regular visits to Farnborough had fostered this idea.

Having given a brief outline of what was involved, the point has been reached whereby individual aspects of the display can now be recorded in more detail, before tying up all loose ends, towards the end of this exercise, and perceive how the whole jig-saw finally fell into place.

For this purpose then I think it is as well to sectionalise the items that had to be dealt with, roughly in the order that we came across them. With the help of a diary I kept of day to day events, I will try to give the reader a picture of how we (the two Johns principally) went about it.

Air Pageant Committee Composition

I am sure the reader will appreciate that it would have been impossible for the two Johns to organise this event entirely on our own, so a sub-committee was formed of members of the club who would be directly concerned with the project. I, for my sins, was elected the chairman. The first meeting of this committee was held as early as March 1969; the final (7th) was held just over a week before the actual event.

Each meeting consisted of a minimum of six (sometimes more) items to be discussed and, when I tell you that not one of these meetings lasted less than two and a half to three hours, one can imagine the amount and complexity of the problems to be discussed and resolved. As it turned out we were indeed fortunate in our selection of a harmonious band of hard working, painstaking individual committee members as a result of which dissent over the more controversial matters became rare and infrequent.

One very important item to be watched over throughout this exercise was the question of finance. Here again, wherever possible we tended to beg, steal or acquire by various means, in order that in the long run, we make the maximum amount of profit with the minimum of outlay. Obviously there were some items that we could not afford to skimp over. For example Insurance, which will be outlined in detail under a separate heading.

On the lighter side, it is worth recording that all these meetings were held in the same venue where the original idea was proposed. So, I think it is safe to say that our thought provoking beverage subsequently helped us over the more awkward moments of our discussions!

One final word concerning the composition of such a committee, we thought it essential that the numbers should be kept to a minimum compatible with the task we had set ourselves, a decision that was to justify itself as time progressed.

The committee consisted of six full time members, including the two Johns, supported regularly by the Club President and Secretary. Again as we were all, without exception, completely new to this kind of exercise, we eventually enlisted the services of the Royal Aero Club who proved invaluable to our needs. When one considers that this organisation is involved annually in a dozen or so Air Displays up and down the countryside, I think it would have been unwise not to have sought their advice, particularly as the event we were organising, and celebrating, was in part connected with this excellent Club.

Having outlined the basic essentials required to add cohesion to our plans, we now proceed further and indicate to the reader the individual items that would collectively fulfil our requirements.

Military Participation

We considered that the RAF would be our main source of 'meat' around which to build the flying programme and in this context, we wrote to the appropriate department in the Ministry of Defence stating our aims and requirements.

The initial reply we received was a little disappointing to say the least. It was to the effect that the "Falcons" the No1 RAF parachute team, albeit good as they are, had been allocated to participate and that, at this stage, was that! Having already tentatively engaged the local Parachute team, we didn't think an Air Display could build around parachuting alone. As a result of this, my colleague took the bull by the horns and telephoned the Ministry of Defence to enquire what else, if any, they would be prepared to provide. To his and my subsequent amazement, they rattled off a number of items, six in all, which included none other than the world renowned 'Red Arrows', the crack RAF Aerobatic Team.

I think it was at this juncture that we really felt our venture was going to be 'all systems go' because without a shadow of doubt, these items alone would be sufficient to attract the public. This proved to be the case. The other item, apart from those mentioned, were a solo Lightning and solo Jet Provost aerobatic aircraft, the famous Battle of Britain fighters, the Spitfire and Hurricane, who were to perform a simulated dog-fight, and lastly as STOL aircraft, the Andover.

After out initial disappointment and subsequent enlightenment from what we considered to be one of the most important telephone calls we made during the whole organising programme, we felt the RAF had done us proud. A factor we shall always be eternally grateful for. I think it is worth mentioning here that the author had at this time, a member of his family who was a Minister in the Government of that period and after having primed him of what we were up to, I believe his discreet enquiries in the right quarters went part way to furthering our cause. This, of course, is a perfect example of string pulling in high places, which can work wonders, and, I make no apologies for using such methods.

This then was the nucleus of our Display but a lot more had to be done in the meantime to bring all these units together on the appropriate day. Suffice it to say the names and addresses of individuals directly concerned with the RAF items were contacted and such things as re-fuelling arrangements, Airport layout and facilities, night stop accommodation etc had all to be arranged and co-ordinated.

In addition to the flying participants, we managed to collar a couple of extra machines, namely a Hercules and another Andover as static exhibits. The acquiring of the Hercules was admittedly, a bit of a 'con' job. Some months previously similar type of aircraft had been allowed into our Airport and the landing fees had been waived. The Commanding Officer of the station the aircraft belonged to, an Air Commodore, was on board and was profuse in his thanks in allowing to be let in free of charge. So, when the time came to think about swelling the static side of our Display, this gentleman was an obvious choice to contact and without hesitation he reacted most favourably.

Apart from the individual addresses we had to contact, copies of our correspondence had to be forwarded to a Squadron Leader, with the grand title of 'RAF co-ordinator' who required all manner of details additional to those mentioned. The reader will now realise why our correspondence reached such mammoth proportions and this was only the beginning! However our attitude towards all this bumph, was that it was worthwhile, bearing in mind what the RAF were prepared to do on our behalf. Of equal importance, was the fact that all they required of us, the organisers, was insurance indemnity and out of pocket expenses. In other words, a very important aspect to bear in mind when organising an event such as this is that if the proceeds are going entirely towards charity, the RAF and the other two services, will gladly participate free of charge, a major consideration in ones budgeting. Also, from the services point of view, there is the added value of free publicity for recruiting which can result from being given the opportunity of displaying their wares to the public on such 'vehicles' as Air Displays.

The Royal Navy provided us respectively with a couple of Sea Vixens and a static mounted Whirlwind helicopter which proved to be extremely popular with the younger element of the crowd on the day itself. Although this aircraft was no longer in flying condition, which is not surprising when one considers the hundreds and thousands who had clambered over it during its countryside recruiting campaigns, all the controls worked and even the rotor blades could be made to turn under ground electrical power. Once again, a piece of useful property for advertising purposes. Regrettably the Army were unable to accommodate us, in the aeronautical sense, but their willingness to try and help knew no bounds.

This then was the military set-up which provided the main backbone of our display. Indeed, without their co-operation, I don't think the venture would have got off the ground literally.

In addition to the three services and whilst on the subject of military participation, further correspondence was entered into with the various manufacturing concerns such as the British Aircraft Corporation, Short Bros., Hawker Siddeley, to name but a few. The majority of these concerns were more or less a 'dead duck' as far as we were concerned; principally because of their involvement in matters of far more importance than merely accommodating comparatively minor functions such as ours.

The main exception was the British Aircraft Corporation. Here for a welcome change, the reply to our standardised letter was, at first glance, very much in the affirmative due, I suspect, to the fact that one of their main factories and associated aerodrome, was virtually on our door step, five miles as the crow flies.

Although neither of us knew the higher-ups in this organisation, once again one of our club members who was the General Manager of the local Evening paper (and ex bomber pilot to boot) knew the Chief Test Pilot. After enlightening this gentleman as to our aims, he in turn advised us the right persons to approach. Of significance was the fact that due to, our respective aerodromes proximity, our 'vehicles', as in the case of the services, would prove to be a useful one which to display their wares and thereby gain useful publicity.

Digressing for a moment, you'll note how often the question of publicity crops up in the narrative. Be that as it may, who were we to complain as long as the prospective 'advertisers' conformed to our wishes.

BAC subsequently proved to be a harder nut to crack than we had envisaged but on being told the facts, the fault did not lie with them, as will be explained.

As a prelude to our enquiries, we were treated to what one might call the 'softening up' process but I hastily add we did not complain at this form of treatment. In other words, we were wined and dined before getting down to the purpose of our visit. Our maim line of approach was to try and obtain one or two of their latest aircraft but I regret, in the long run, this was not to be. Unfortunately, unknown to us at the material time, the aircraft they had were not in fact owned by the manufacturer; they were either under HM Government control or had already been earmarked for some foreign power. So that put paid to those ideas. Although we appreciated that there was nothing BAC could do about this aspect of our display, nevertheless it was regrettable that having obtained an aircraft representative of the early days of aviation, more of this later, we had hoped to complement it by acquiring an aircraft representing the opposite end of the scale, namely the most up to date military hardware, for example the Jaguar. However, this was not to be and there was no point in crying over spilt milk. Before leaving this subject and just to show we were not chicken hearted, we even ventured to enquire of the possibility of Concorde appearing (admittedly with tongue in cheek!). Not surprising, it didn't work. At least we tried.

Nevertheless all was not lost. Looking at the brighter side, the static aspect of their representation almost compensated for the absence of their flying machines. This included a Jet Provost with all its attendant armoury neatly displayed around it, a very attractive and well laid out exhibit! The second item they provided, at considerable cost to themselves I might add, was a huge marquee containing all manner of aeronautical 'goodies' displayed for the public's amusement and interest. Included in this exhibition marquee was a beautiful scale model of the Concorde, at least we obtained the model of the ultimate even if it wasn't the real thing! As an indication of its size, it had to be transported on an R.A.F. 'Queen Mary' trailer, and weighed more than a ton into the bargain. In conclusion the BAC did us proud and the crowd took full advantage of the facilities provided. At all events, not a bad days work on a free meal and drinks ticket!

Finally, to complete the list of organisations we thought would be prepared to assist us, the other John approached that well-known restorer of aviation products, the Shuttleworth collection. Principally the idea of contacting them was to try and obtain a Vintage aircraft in flying condition, representative of the era we were, in part commemorating. Although I had been to this very worthwhile place before, purely as a spectator, I was now approaching them in the role of a 'Sprog' Air Display organiser.

Apart from an opportunity to avail myself once again of a further detailed study of their numerous exhibits, I was able to ascertain what they had to offer and a number of recommended items were duly noted for our consideration. We eventually selected an Avro Tutor (vintage 1931) which was the nearest we could get to the actual year we were commemorating. We subsequently heard that this was one of their finest flying exhibits so we were well satisfied with our temporary 'purchase'. This was one of the few occasions whereby an item had to be hired for our display but, in this case, when one realises that the Shuttleworth trust relies almost entirely on public funds for its existence, we felt the money was going towards a worthwhile cause.

In the final event, regrettably this aircraft never reached us from its home base due to fog, which blanketed most of the Southern part on the U.K. on the 18th October 1969.

Incidentally it is as well to point out here that where expenditure in connection with our Air Pageant was concerned, I had to refer such matters to my colleague. He was senior to me in the hierarchy of the club we belonged to, quite apart from the fact that he was chairman of that particular club service which organised events to raise money for charity. Perhaps this gives one a clearer picture of why the two of us were able to work in such close harmony, admirably supported by our committee. As we were both actively engaged in the aviation profession, myself through my position as the Senior Air Traffic Controller and my colleague as a qualified private pilot. Basically he was a businessman in the Painting and Decorating trade, aviation being his pet hobby. So we were able to steer our committee along the right lines due to our interest and basic knowledge of the aviation world in general.

We now reckoned that we had taken care of both ends of the aviation life span so to speak so, all we had to do now flying wise, was provide the 'padding' in between, hence the reason for considering civil participation.

Civil Participation

As in case of Farnborough, which everyone directly or indirectly connected with aviation knows about, we surmised that a true Air Display must be a combination of Military and civil aeronautical equipment, in order to cater for the individual tastes of the public at large. In this context, we were fortunate in having a branch of one of the larger Independent Airlines based on our doorstep.

Of equal importance, as far as I was concerned, was that I was 'well-in' with the Chief Pilot and Chief Training Captain which enabled me to cajole them into complying with my wishes.

The airline had a fleet of Dart Herald aircraft and I managed to persuade the aforementioned gentlemen to allocate one of their aircraft as a static exhibit, the other to take part in the flying display itself. The flying exhibit would be piloted by the training captain, a person I had had the privilege of flying with on numerous occasions during my own flying career. He more than lived up to my expectations by executing a brilliant party piece on the day in question, even if as I subsequently heard, he did frighten himself silly in the process! I must admit that rarely have I witnessed a civil airliner being flown with such panache, particularly the extremely low fly-past aspect of his display. No wonder it cost me a couple of pints later on that evening!

Apart from providing display aircraft, one had to remember that the company had to continue with its routine scheduled services and here again we learnt another cardinal rule whereby when one organises such 'does' at Airports having regular scheduled services, these schedules must on no account be interfered with. In other words, whereas we were permitted to temporarily suspend all other aviation activities prior, during and for a period of time after the display, scheduled services were the exception to this flying restriction. So, when we came to the point where we had to draft out a display programme, these extra flights had to be fitted in at the times indicated in their timetable and consequently a certain amount of juggling about was necessary in order to permit these particular flights to proceed unhindered. It must now be obvious to would-be Air Display organisers that when selecting a venue for such an exercise, try and pick somewhere where there is little or no scheduled service activity! You'd be surprised at how few U.K. licensed Airports there are without this facility so, naturally ones choice of venue tends to be somewhat limited. For example, one would have no chance of organising such an event at say London (Heathrow) where scheduled services are a form of continuous air display in itself. Similarly this would apply at Manchester (Ringway) or other busy Airports. With hindsight then, another useful lesson learnt, see what I mean by pitfalls and frustrations!

Other aspects of our civil contribution were provided by the three resident flying clubs whom, although not particularly well versed in the finer art of display performing. We nonetheless felt obliged to extend invitations considering that we were contemplating disrupting most of their activities for the majority of that particular Saturday which, after all from a commercial point of view, was one of their more lucrative days of the week. Here again, another lesson was learnt in so much that any prospective air display performers should be allowed sufficient time, before the event itself, to practise their performance. Yet another item that had escaped out attention until it was almost too late.

Whilst on the subject of this aspect of light aviation, we were approached by a group of private enthusiasts who aptly came under the title of the 'Barnstormers'. Unfortunately they applied too late for us to fit them into our programme which was remiss on our part because they do put on a very good show. This was subsequently proved, at a later date, when they did perform at this Airport. Indeed they perform all over the country. The only saving grace as far as we were concerned was that, had we included them in our plans, it would have extended our flying display into darkness. At this time of the year, night time falls pretty early. As it was, the flying programme didn't end until near darkness, it being all of three hours in duration, which is comparable to the length of a Farnborough display. In passing, the Barnstormers full display programme takes all of two and half-hours and is of particular interest to the Private/Sporting pilot fraternity.

Of the other civil representation, there were a number of business/Executive aircraft that performed in their own inimitable way.

As starters prior to the flying programme commencing, we had an excellent demonstration by the local radio controlled flying model society whose detailed scale models, coupled with their flying capability in the expert hands of their dedicated owners, had to be seen to be appreciated.

This virtually completed the 'padding' which is so vitally necessary if one is hoping to produce an interesting and varied programme.

Before going onto the question of the civil static exhibition, there was one other civil participant of note which, had it come off, would have been quite a feather in our cap. As mentioned earlier, we had enlisted the services of the Royal Aero Club and their Secretary General, acting on our behalf, had offered the Zlin aircraft which was earmarked for the forthcoming world aerobatics championships. This aircraft was sponsored by Players Gold Leaf, which, to my way of thinking, would be a way of recruiting a ready-made sponsor to further promote our efforts.

All previous attempts at trying to enlist the services of a sponsor had failed.

One might ask, in what way could they have helped our venture? Principally in the realm of publicity. For example, they offered to supply posters, car stickers, advertisements in local papers, programme inserts, etc, which to use their own words '.... Will help to reduce your committee's financial burdens and will demonstrate the positive contribution Gold leaf wish to make to further public interest in air displays.' Incidentally, no mention was made at this stage, of financial advantage in terms of hard cash, from which we would have benefited.

One can imagine my consternation when I presented these facts to our committee for their approval and after considerable deliberation they, in their wisdom, turned the offer down! I think they were afraid that this additional publicity would lessen the impact, from a publicity point of view, that this was a Rotary organised venture. I could not for the life of me understand this attitude as I looked upon this offer as a valuable contribution towards 'spreading the word' around much further than we were able to do and thereby enhance the reputation of our movement, backed by a household named product. However, the committee was adamant, so I had no alternative but to accede their wishes.

It is fair to say that this was the only time during the whole of the organising process that there was a major discord between the committee and myself.

Nevertheless not to be put off, the Royal Aero Club did provide us with I similar aircraft (for which we had to pay) and which was to prove quite an attraction as it was piloted by one of the British Aerobatics team members, namely Charles Black. In retrospect, one admittedly has to very careful over the question of sponsorship, and resulting publicity, as there is a distinct danger of the would be sponsor 'stealing the thunder' from the original organisers although I was not aware this danger at the time.

It's amazing what one learns when undertaking such a mammoth exercise as ours! In order to complete the full circle concerning civil aviation participation, and having already persuaded the local airline to show its flag, it occurred to us that rarely are the Civilian airlines ever represented at air displays. I suppose this is not really suprising because an aircraft lying motionless on the ground is costing its operator money. Despite this obvious fact, we let enthusiasm run away with us and accordingly further stereotyped letters were duly despatched to fifteen independent Airlines requesting their support in either the flying and/or static configuration. We had previously been advised that the two Corporations, BOAC and BEA were too heavily committed and therefore would not be in a position to help us.

Before going onto how the Independents reacted we did, with tongue in cheek, approach of all people, the Russian Airline Aeroflot. This suggestion came from one of the committee members who remembered that some years previously the then Russian Ambassador to this country had been invited to switch on our towns famous Illuminations, sometimes described as the 'Greatest free show on earth!' After he had performed this ceremony and during the ensueing reception, he had been overheard to remark that if at some future date he could in any way be of assistance, he would be delighted to help, hence our reason for approaching his country's national airline.

The upshot of this enquiry and bearing in mind that we were fully aware that the USSR did not recognise our movement, we had again fallen short of the time element; maybe we didn't help our cause by wrongly addressing the letter in the first place! Nevertheless it is worth recording that we did eventually receive a very courteous reply, which was to the effect that if we had approached them sooner, they might well have been interested in doing something for us. One further reason for making this approach was that we had heard the Russians were rather partial to parading their wares in any country that in the long run might benefit them from a sales point of view. One thing, it did prove to us that where there's a will there's a way and for future amateur air display organisers, don't hesitate to spread your tentacles far and wide.

One company we were fortunate enough to approach was Britannia Airways who happened to be positioning a Boeing 737 into Blackpool on the day prior to our display. So it wasn't difficult to persuade them to allow us to put their aircraft on the area allocated to static exhibits. It proved to be a very attractive exhibit with a constant stream of people waiting to see the 'innards' throughout the time the airport was open to the public, so much so that I believe the two hostesses on board were almost overwhelmed by the sheer weight of numbers.

As regards the other companies we wrote to, the only response was a half promise of a BAC 1-11 and a definite promise of the ubiquitous DC3 belonging to an Irish independent.

We were naturally disappointed at this apparent lack of interest but one has to accept the facts as outlined.

Our final static line up, which just about filled the area we had reserved for this purposed, was as follows. The Boeing 737, Hercules, Andover and the resident airline's Herald. The DC3 didn't turn up after all; we never did find out the reason why. This may not appear very much at first glance but when one considers that all these aircraft were fully open to the public, they were sufficient in numbers to keep a large section of the crowd occupied.

This then constituted our static and flying display participation. Perhaps a word or two now concerning the miscellaneous items offered to us without which this story would be incomplete.

Miscellaneous Items

During the course of our programming we learnt of an interesting exhibition being held at Manchester airport to celebrate the first Atlantic crossing by those adventurous Englishmen Alcock and Brown in their Vickers Vimy bi-plane. The main point of interest in this exhibition, as far as we were concerned, was a beautiful full-scale flying replica of their Vimy, housed in an inflated plastic tent. There were other exhibits too, but the replica was what specially attracted our attention. After arranging a suitable time and place to meet the Manchester Corporation Public Relations Officer who was principally concerned in this exhibition, we set of from our homesteads to do business, or at least we hoped to.

This gentleman met us and duly gave us a personally conducted tour. Our focal point of interest, the replica, more than lived up to expectations and we made a mental note there and then to see what we could do in order to acquire it for our own display. Preliminary investigations were entered into with the owners of this machine, Vintage Aircraft Ltd., but it looked as though the main stumbling block would be the cost of hiring this valuable piece of equipment (it cost Manchester Corporation £3000 to hire it for one month!). As it turned out, our answer was provided by the untimely demise that befell this machine three days later when, on a particularly hot day, the sun's rays penetrated the plastic 'hangar' setting fire to the Vimy. It was extensively damaged, so that put paid to any further thoughts we had in that direction.

However, despite the fact that we didn't achieve anything, it was a pleasant day's outing with expenses paid, meal and drinks thrown in for good measure!

Once again the odd perks we enjoyed more than made up for our occasional disappointments; it wasn't a case of 'all work and no play makes Jack a dull boy'. We did have our compensations.

The only other exhibit of note was offered to us by a group of enthusiasts known as the Northern Aircraft Preservation Society. They offered, and we accepted, two of their restored aircraft (trailer mounted) namely an Avro Avian and the amazing pre-war Flying Flea. They certainly helped to swell our ground borne attractions.

As one can imagine, numerous trade organisations applied for rights to display their wares but we ruled out all those that had no aeronautical flavour which, in actual fact, just about ruled out the lot! The exception was a mobile aviation bookshop that contained, apart from aviation magazines, other items of interest to the aviation minded.

Oh yes, one other concern that I should have mentioned was the USAF. For the initiated of our movement, Rotary International was founded in that country and therefore it was only natural that we should make overtures in that direction. The author, through his acquaintance with the ex-meteorological Chief at the airport, whom I knew to be well-in with the American Air Force Headquarters personnel in London, strenuously endeavoured, on our behalf to, inveigle the Americans to participate. Alas after many letters and phone calls, the enquiries came to nought. To be fair to them, this was the year they were celebrating some important event in their history so all their armed services were committed one way and another, in the interests of their own country folk.

This just about winds up the participation aspect of our venture and therefore having created the 'Pinnacle' of our mountainous exercise, we now had to ensure that the whole exercise was well and truly 'shored-up'. In other words the flying display itself would not flounder due to insufficient back-up arrangements, barring the ever-present threat of adverse weather. Before going onto what I have called the shoring-up process, let us consider the all-important question of Insurance.

Insurance and Legal Requirements

This must of necessity, be one of the most important aspects of an Air Display organiser's itinerary. The importance can be gauged by the fact that out of all our expenditure, this one single item was by far the largest, six to seven hundred pounds.

In the first place, the R.A.F. and the RN require a large indemnity (half a million pounds to be exact). Then there was our own employers who owned the Airport and who required third party coverage to the tune of three million pounds, just for the one day of the display. It is interesting to note that this coverage is the 'norm' for one complete year! On top of this there were other comparatively minor items needing insurance cover, the most important of which we, the organisers, would be covered in the event of the display being cancelled due to weather. This coverage was called the 'No Go' or Abandonment policy, which meant that on the day itself, a time limit was set before which we could cancel the display if it became necessary and consequently all our overheads, would be reimbursed. At least our heads wouldn't roll if the worst came to the worst!

Originally it was thought that the resources within our own organisation would be adequate to pay the premiums; in other words, it was thought best to keep insurance 'in the family'. Subsequently though they realised that this aspect of our requirements would best be served by outside insurance agencies who would be familiar with what was needed..

Again we had been fortuitous because the insurers who eventually accommodated us were indeed highly experienced in events such as ours. For example they looked after needs of the annual R.A.F.A. Woodford display, which is rapidly becoming the 'Farnborough of the North'. So we are assured of the right kind of guidance in this all-important requirements.

Like many other items that had to be tackled, the initial approach, done through a very personable young representative of the insurance brokers we had been advised to contact, was the completion of what seemed at first sight, a formidable questionnaire. I think it is true to say that many a person is often frightened off by such documents, but when expert advice is to hand, such as we were fortunate to have, somehow the questions become more reasonable to the uninitiated, and prove in the long run to be relatively straightforward. Digressing for a moment, form filling is one aspect of everyday life that I abhor and am always glad of any opportunity to 'palm-off' to the more clerical minded of our community. The completion of this questionnaire was virtually the basis upon which all our requirements would be finalised and suffice it to say that all these were met by various deadlines stipulated by the Airport owners and the Military. Furthermore policies were subsequently issued to show we meant business. Items to be covered and individual premium amounts were as follows:

A	Blackpool Corporation indemnity (for £3,000,000)	£250
B	Crown indemnity (for £250,000)	£90
C	Public liability	£250
D	Personal accident (for voluntary helpers)	£35
E	No Go/Abandonment	£35
F	Cash in transit	£10
G	Sundry other items	£21
	TOTAL	£691

I must admit that quite a few eye-brows were raised at the amount involved but any misgivings were quickly dispelled by pointing out the facts of life which were simply No insurance, No display – fait accompli.

It is interesting to note that this particular part of our total expenditure outlay was the only one that had to be paid before the event; the others, mercifully, were not demanded until after the exercise had taken place.

Our club, like all others, did have certain reserves to cope with contingencies such as we proposed and although they were stretched to the limit, there was no need to resort to such drastic methods as 'raiding the bank'. No doubt had we resorted to such methods, our Bank Manager members might have been persuaded to turn a 'blind eye' to such goings on!

I have been purposely brief in this part of the narrative as no doubt one would agree that this could be a boring subject if gone into in great detail but nevertheless it's an item that one cannot afford to leave out.

Domestic Arrangements – (Shoring-up Process)

Apart from the actual flying display itself, this was possibly our biggest hurdle and could be likened to a pedestal upon which the Pinnacle of the display would be built.

The correct term for this exercise s contained in the circular 'Safety arrangements at Air Displays' which I have mentioned in a previous chapter. For amateurs such as us, it proved to be an invaluable guideline as to what was required. Amongst the major requirements were such things as crowd barriers, fire, ambulance and doctor coverage, public address system, etc, all of which highlighted the magnitude of the task we had set ourselves, but undaunted we went ahead!

Possibly the best way of explaining what was involved is to briefly go through the circular, item by item, and let you see how ultimately we were able to resolve each stage as it cropped up. Although we were still in the relatively primary stage of reaching our objective, all the following had to be organised well in advance of 'D' day in order that the whole 'jig-saw puzzle' could be put together during the week immediately preceding the event.

Item 1 – Crowd Barriers – This is where my colleague with his connections in the building trades came into his own. He was able to persuade, and believe me he could be persuasive if he was in right mood, a scaffolding firm to provide us with what was supposed to be a 'Farnborough' type of barrier. I say supposed to be because we were never able to get a clear cut answer as to what constituted a Farnborough barrier. However as the Board of Trade and our insurers approved of our choice, who were we to complain!

We measured out the distance involved and, to show how deceptive the area of an Airport can be, the final coverage for this one item alone came to a staggering two miles! My colleague's persuasiveness even extended to getting the complete job done for nothing, a remarkable feat! Our maxim of beg, borrow or otherwise acquire, was paying off handsomely. Nothing like having connections in the right quarters.

Once having organised this particular item, the actual preparation and eventual layout took almost a week to complete. It was as well that we didn't leave this exercise until the last moment!

Following upon this, one naturally progresses to the next item on the 'menu'.

Item 2 – Crowd Control – This as was fondly thought, was to prove to be a major exercise, particularly in the number of personnel involved. Two miles is quite a length to patrol.

This is where one of our more distinguished members, the head of Police, entered the limelight. He collared virtually the whole of the local police force, thereby denuding the populace of its 'men in blue.' The local criminal fraternity could have had a field day if they had but known the freedom they were being offered! This same gentleman was also amongst the hierarchy in the local and area ATC cadet force and through him, their services were offered and eagerly snapped up. Their eventual involvement on our behalf was not only in keeping the crowd within the spectator areas delineated by the crowd barrier, no mean task in itself, but they were also responsible for preventing the public from clambering over such expensive machinery as the Folland Gnats of the 'Red Arrows'. One can see then that there was no lack of supervisory duties to be undertaken; all part of the necessary 'oiling of the cog wheels' to ensure the smooth running of the entire operation. As is the case in any large public spectacle, there is the ever-present threat of accidents or injuries involving either the flying display participants themselves, or members of the public. God forbid that an organiser should have a major disaster on his hands but, like everything else, one must be prepared for such eventualities and therefore the next item is again a natural progression form one stage to the next.

Item 3 – FIRE SERVICES, AMBULANCES AND DOCTORS- These three very necessary safety aspects of our display were organised by the appropriate professional in our club, and neighbouring clubs who had a vested interest in our efforts. This is a further example whereby we were able to draw upon resources within our ranks whereas, other potential organisers of Air Displays, might have to search far and wide for professional people necessary for such duties and, what is more, have to pay for their services considerably in excess of what we had to.

I often refer to this question of expense but, at the risk of being accused a miser and repeating myself, this was one of the many 'parcels of essentials' we were able to tie up with the minimum of financial outlay. However, to continue, detailed orders were eventually produced, and selected vantage points were allocated to our safety services on the field of operations, having already obtained the necessary approval from the powers that be.

Incidentally, as an off-shoot of the foregoing and an equally important safety contingency, was the provision of a lost children's tent. This 'chore' was undertaken by one of our Reverend members and there is a delightful picture of him standing outside the tent holding a large placard scribed 'Lost Children' which, as some wag suggested, would have been complete if the signwriter had missed out the last three letters of the word 'Children'. Fortunately our Reverend friend had a great sense of humour.

Up to now no mention has been made of the numbers of personnel involved in the foregoing items of our domestic arrangements. In order to convey some idea of the scale of our operations, the following facts are an integral part of any Air Display. Largely as the result of an on-the-site inspection and detailed discussions of personnel deployment, we arrived at a basic man-power requirement of 280 persons, deployed as follows: -

100 Police cadets
60 ATC Cadets
100 Scouts
20 Scouts- programme selling

The last item was originally the responsibility of 20 young ladies from the local Polish Air Forces Club, dressed in National costume. Unfortunately the idea fell through; a pity because we felt the feminine guile would have boosted our programme selling no end, no disrespect to the scouts intended! As a supplement to the above numbers there were members of our own club, members of other Rotary clubs, and local Round Tablers who were employed in such duties as car and coach parking, manning entrance turnstiles, and general crowd control duties. Inevitably loop-holes appeared in our carefully prepared arrangements and so this additional man-power plugged them where they occurred. All in all then, when one considers that all available airport employees were also utilised in various capacities, we must have finished up with more like 400 persons dispersed throughout the display site. Of note, each individual received a circular prepared by myself, detailed rendezvous and vantage points to be covered, and specific duties required of the individuals.

As to the numbers covering the safety arrangements i.e. Fire, Police, Ambulance and Doctors, the foremost was the largest single item (apart from the Police) as can be judged by the following; -

6 Fire Tenders including an overall control unit

with their respective personnel. These were additional to the

Airport's own fire service - say 30 to 40 persons all told.

These appliances were placed at strategic points adjacent the display runway, the Control unit being placed alongside the Air Traffic Control tower for ease of communication.

Finally to complete the list of safety personnel required there were two Ambulances plus their crews, and two Doctors, one being a Rotary club member. Worthy of mention is that, had there been a major incident, the foregoing on-site safety services would have been supplemented by their respective outside agencies, which including the local hospitals, had already been forewarned of our activities.

The next item brings us to the question of communications which one can appreciate is vitally necessary when such a large area has to be covered by individuals spread thinly but strategically throughout it, not forgetting of course the importance of keeping the public informed about the proceedings, as and when they occurred.

Item 4 – Public Address System – It has often been said that the public address system (PA system for short) of any outdoor event can make or mar the effectiveness of the entertainment value given to the spectators at large. Naturally it must be backed up by a good commentary, more of this later. I can personally comment on the validity of this statement, being an avid Motor Racing fan, a form of sport where I consider the hearing of what's going on more than complements what the eye can see. The ultimate in achieving a satisfactory balance between the two connecting factors of such a system, boils down to the strategic placing of the poles carrying the amplifiers which ideally should be directed towards the spectators in every direction possible.

In any case because of the area involved and the limited budget we had at our disposal, we tended to spread our tentacles over a wider area than was subsequently found to have been necessary. I hasten to add that this was basically our own fault and is no reflection on the company, which provided us with this service. Suffice to say that had we known beforehand where the majority of the crowd would be concentrated, we could have provided a better coverage. Nevertheless, for those members of the public, and our erstwhile volunteers, who enjoyed exceptional hearing or were standing into 'wind' there was certainly value for money!

It is interesting to note that, like the erection of the crowd barrier, the PA system also took a week to install. The net result of the latter was rather reminiscent of wartime Britain whereby, you may recall, all large fields were staked out with substantial poles ostensibly to ward off any potential airborne aggressor. Obviously this wasn't the purpose of our exercise but nevertheless, there was a striking resemblance!

In addition to all this, the whole shooting match had somehow or other to be connected up to a focal point namely the control tower, which, not unnaturally, became the hub of all communications directly concerned with the display. This was quite an exercise in itself. All relevant cabling has to be threaded into a miniature control console, something like the railway lines converging on to Clapham junction! At this juncture, the whole job lot would have been completely useless without the services of a Commentator so we come to yet another item of progression in our narrative.

Item 5 – The Commentator – The preamble to Item 4 is equally true in relation to the acquisition of a good commentator, who apart from the flying spectacular itself, is a mainstay of the public's interest, particularly where through unforeseen circumstances, gaps appear in the programme and he has to 'fill-in'. In other words, what a display organiser is looking for is not only a person who knows his subject inside out but he must also be something of a raconteur. Now the question arises, how does one go about finding the right person who combines these two essential qualities? It's not an easy hurdle to overcome. We had by this stage of the proceedings committed ourselves irrevocably, so such headaches, important as they were, would not be allowed to develop into neuralgia! Therefore soundings were made in what we thought would be the right quarters. After one or two shots directed towards well known personalities in this field of entertainment, which we openly admit, were pure 'shots in the dark', we were not unduly daunted when we received blank refusals to our overture, albeit very courteous refusals.

Then, as so often happens in such circumstances, the answer virtually materialised on our own doorstep. One of the resident flying clubs had as its President a certain well known Radio and TV personality and, as luck would have it, this gentleman was a personal friend of one our local airlines pilots. Through the latter's offices, we not only managed to obtain the services of our unsuspecting commentator, despite his considerably entertainment engagements but, of equal importance, he volunteered his services free; a most welcome gesture. Apart from his Radio and TV fame whereby his considerably girth and statue made him instantly recognisable, he had been a wartime pilot complete with DFC. He still maintained an interest in aviation so his aeronautical knowledge was more than adequate for the task we had set him. Also, he owned his own light aircraft in which he flew from one engagement to another. Perhaps a little digression here would be appropriate to indicate his brand of humour, aviation wise. Some months previously he had arrived at our Airport in somewhat adverse weather conditions, in order to take part in a show biz spectacular. Having spent some time in the air unsuccessfully trying to locate the Airport visually, he eventually resorted to 'homing' by the use of D/ F bearings, a considerably less accurate letdown aid than the all-important seeing eye of Radar. At that time we did not have this facility. However our comedian friend, not to be outdone, included in his act (which was broadcast live) an amusing sketch whereby he twiddled his music stand several times before proclaiming that this was what was lacking at this particular Airport. I've often wondered how we obtained this vital piece of equipment, without which most Airports are severely handicapped! Incidentally, by now the reader should have adequate clues as to his identity. Good as our selected personage was we realised that it would be imposing an unnecessary burden on him to carry out a continuous commentary for three and half to four hours. So, the question of selecting a suitable back-up commentator was quite easily solved when I recalled that my original contact man was quite a raconteur in his own right, albeit mainly over drinks in a bar, which inevitably enlivened the company he was keeping. Anyway quick as a flash, I thought to myself, he's done me a good turn so why not reciprocate by offering him this additional post.

He initial reply to my invitation was unprintable, but I'm glad to say, he did accept and made a splendid job of it. Just as I fondly thought he would! How to win friends and influence people! To conclude this part of the organisation, the night before the event, what was supposed to be a pre-briefing exercise, turned into being a near riot whereby our guest commentator regaled us with jokes and anecdotes which became so hilarious (and blue) that the original purpose of the exercise was completely over-looked. Just as well our lady companions had by this time discreetly left our company and moved into more sedate surroundings! Suffice to say that the commentary, despite the apparent lack of preparation, did go down very well. No doubt the sheer personality of the gentleman concerned had something to do with the overall presentation of what I have already indicated was a very necessary part of our exercise.

The next item on the agenda is what I call the overall air to ground/ground to air radio link, that is Air Traffic Control, which emanated from my little 'empire', the Control Tower.

Item 6 – Air Traffic Control – From a spectator point of view, Air Traffic Control is not immediately apparent as a necessary part of an air display. But from an organisers viewpoint, apart from the fact that it is a mandatory requirement by the Civil Aviation authorities, it does 'knit' together the actual flying display itself thereby providing the public with the kind of spectacle they have come to expect.

One obvious example of the value of Air Traffic Control is the co-ordination it provides between each individual flying participant. As is so admirably demonstrated at Farnborough, where, entirely due to detailed prior planning and subsequent control of the display by the controller himself, the spectacle becomes rather like a conveyer belt of continuous flying where say a maximum time 'slot' between each event is of the order of 30 seconds or less. I think you will appreciate that this is a pretty tight time schedule to adhere to.

Other aspects of Air Traffic Control involvement are in such matters as Air to ground frequency selection, controlling all traffic within the immediate vicinity of the Airport, irrespective of its purpose, attending the briefing prior to the display pointing out obstructions, hazards, routings, etc., etc. Now to the question as to whose shoulders this responsibility would fall upon. As I was tied up with organising this 'Bonanza' I would not have time to act as the display controller, how easily one is able to wriggle out of awkward situations! so I resorted to the well known system of asking for volunteers – you, you and you. Seriously though I was fortunate that my number two, or Deputy if that sounds more impressive, volunteered without hesitation and, in the course of time, I was indeed fortunate in my volunteer who was, and always has been, an imperturbable character. He more than lived up to his reputation, a very necessary ingredient of any controller was undertaking such a responsibility. One has to bear in mind that he had never been involved in such an exercise before, it being a somewhat different aspect of his duties compared to what is considered normal. Despite this he contributed in no small way towards the ultimate success of the display and I would venture to say that he actually enjoyed this unusual role he was asked to perform.

Needless to say Pete was suitably rewarded for services rendered, by being invited to not only the previous recorded riotous 'booze-up', but also to a similar 'shindig' laid on after the event, where a mutual admiration society blossomed!

This then really concludes the abbreviated version of what was principally involved on the domestic side of our project but, before proceeding further, it is worth recording that there were other varied details to be tided up. Allocation of car and coach parking areas, toilet facilities, the latter an item that somehow always seems lacking at any one day outdoor event and I regret to say, ours was no exception. Positioning of refreshment marquees, the catering was in the hands of the Airport concessionaires, so that was one headache we didn't have to bother about.

One aspect I have so far omitted to mention was the question of a map that had to be prepared and distributed to all interested parties, after the necessary approval had been obtained. This indicated the entire ground layout annotated with such items as the crowd barrier delineation, car/coach parking areas, toilet locations etc., not forgetting the all important indication from the spectators point of view, the alignment of the display runway where all the fun and games would be happening! Once again the preparation of this map was undertaken by yet another club member who was the area Engineer of the North Western Electricity Board and who, in turn, 'persuaded' his drawing office to make the required number of copies. This proved no mean feat when one considers that all this work was done at nil cost. Under normal circumstances, these maps would have involved considerable expense, as anyone connected with the printing and cartographic trade will tell you.

I recall that we ended up with fifty copies of the original map and even then, there were none to spare.

The Royal Aero Club

I realise that I have mentioned this organisation previously but, as they were going to be intimately involved in our affairs, I think it is worth devoting a short separate chapter outlining why they became involved. In the Department of Trade and Industry's circular I have indicated their recommendation in seeking this club's assistance as they are well versed in the innumerable problems associated with the organisation of air displays. Consequently due contact was made with their Secretary General, Simon Ames, who proved to be most helpful. Of academic interest, when I eventually met him in person, I was somewhat surprised by his apparent youthfulness as I expected to meet a more elderly person, considering the high position he held in this renowned club! Furthermore, at that time I was not aware of his aviation background although it was obvious from his appearance that he would have been too young to have been involved actively in the last war. Subsequently I did ascertain that he had been a Fleet Air arm Jet pilot and presumably his organising talents had been recognised prior to his entry into the somewhat different field of civil aviation, with particular emphasis on light aircraft actively i.e. private and club flying. In my letters to the Secretary General, I indicated amongst other things, our aims and the specific aspect of those aims where I thought the Club's assistance would be required.

As a follow up, an appointment was made for me to visit the headquarters of the Royal Aero Club in London; the other John was otherwise occupied on this occasion.

This was yet another occasion where the fruits of ones labours became pleasure in so much that it meant a break from routine for a day return trip to London by rail, accompanied by my briefcase, which was beginning to show signs of bursting at the seams.

My particular concern was the format of the actual flying display itself and its timing. I had already drafted out a provisional flying programme which, much to my surprise, was not considered to be such a clumsy attempt, as I had at first feared. Simon, our Royal Aero Club mentor studied this and other aspects of our proposed display, at some length, and subsequently promised wholehearted support.

At this junction the reader should appreciate that under normal circumstances, enlisting the aid of such an august body as the Royal Aero Club would cost the organisers a not inconsiderable amount in professional fees. But here, because the nature of our exercise was in part connected with the Royal Aero club, and also using the now well worn phrase 'limited funds', the Royal Aero Club and in particular Simon, its Secretary General, very kindly offered the club's services for a nominal sum. It goes without saying that we certainly had our money's worth!

As I have said, what bothered me most was the actual programming of the flying display and I was never more thankful than when Simon undertook to look after this particular problem on our behalf. Not only did he do this long before we were in a position to tie up loose ends, but he actually came up for the display itself, together with his charming secretary, who was a model of efficiency. His unquestionable organising talents really came out into the open, as will be seen from the following.

Inevitably any organiser suffers from last minute cancellation of specific items, which in turn can throw the whole flying programme completely out of gear. We were no exception. In fact, this was precisely the sort of 'disaster' I dreaded most. Simon took all this last minute 'panic' as a matter of routine and without hesitation, altered the entire programme in less than thirty minutes before the start of the display.

Before going on further, it is only fair to say that almost all the last minute cancellations were due entirely to our old adversary the weather. For example, three items, namely the Spitfire, Hurricane and Avro Tutor, became fog-bound at their home bases. The Lightning rendered itself unserviceable prior to its departure for our show.

However, getting back to the point in question, not only did the whole programme have to be re-timed, which in itself was quite a feat, but the time intervals between each item had to be maintained in order that the public could still enjoy a continuous, uninterrupted programme. In addition, this revised programme had to be distributed to participants, the commentator, and other interested parties.

This is where Simon's secretary proved her worth, particularly as there was a last minute panic to try and locate a Roneo duplicating machine. Eventually I managed to 'borrow' one from the locally based Airline.

The second reason whereby Simon's expertise proved its worth was in keeping an eagle eye on my number two's handling, or rather controlling of the display. This was of inestimable value to Pete.

To sum up then, we indeed had been fortunate in acquiring the services of an organisation who are acknowledged experts in this role of aviation activity. For the price paid, the dividend return was high. I would without hesitation, recommend the Royal Aero Club to any 'would be' regular air display organiser, even if they have to pay the full fee normally charged for such services, as we did indeed for our second air display: however that is another story.

Publicity

Any project which needs to be brought to the attention of the public must, for obvious reasons, be directed in such a manner that the fullest impact is made in the right quarters. This is easier said than done unless one has unlimited resources. This was not so in our case. Nevertheless this particular aspect of our venture was almost as important as obtaining the right amount of participants and in the final analysis, the costs of publicising the display proved to be our second largest item of expenditure.

We were indeed fortunate that the club member who undertook this not inconsiderable task, is in the printing trade and therefore his advertising knowledge became invaluable in directing our efforts along the right lines. Without going into the intricate details of all that was involved (this alone would constitute a separate story) perhaps the odd example of how we went about publicising our proposed venture will indicate to the reader the enormity of the task we had set our printing colleague.

In the first instance, 20,000 handbills were printed giving brief details of the air display. These were distributed not only locally to the Town Hall, Hotels, Boarding houses, Schools etc. but also to a number of long distance coach companies whom we fondly thought we would be spreading the "message" far and wide. On reflection, we wondered if we had miss-cued on this novel idea of ours. Maybe we would have been better off if we had spread the word around the densely populated areas within say, a 200-mile radius of the Airport.

However, having decided upon our overall policy, we couldn't very well change horses in midstream and so our deliberations were acted upon. As it turned out, once the message had begun to spread, enquiries from sources other than those already covered began to come in a steady stream, so much so that our erstwhile printer ended up printing a further 10,000 of the self same bills, and this was only the beginning!

Apart from the distribution of handbills, we had to consider those aviation magazines best known to the enthusiasts to whom air displays act as a magnet. Basically one has to cater for two types of person who feel it worthwhile patronising such "do's", even if it means travelling fairly long distances. The first kind is the enthusiast who will come from far and wide and who quite rightly, demands value for money. Therefore one has to give the impression that a first class display will be put on for their benefit irrespective of the apparent shambles gong on behind the scenes. There were times when it appeared that our organisational progress was nothing but a shambles.

The second kind of person one has to cater for is the ordinary man, woman and child in the street, who whilst not particularly interested in, would still be expecting a good show.

I have deliberately pointed out the type of customer one has to coerce into attending such events as it must give a clearer picture of how far one has to go on this vital aspect of advertising.

I almost forgot to mention that amongst the handbill distribution list was every flying club in the country, which totalled 193.

The other prime activities in this particular field came in the final few weeks before the big day itself, whereby advertisements were placed in the local newspapers at regular intervals, in order that maximum impact could be brought to bear upon the unsuspecting populace! Additionally, posters were displayed at strategic vantage points around town and on the approaches to it. Incidentally, these latter two exercises required an imaginative brain quorum from the Air Display committee, as their design and format had to be such that the pictorial and written presentation of such advertising media would command more than just a casual look, a good exercise in public relations!

Referring back to the advertising with long distance coach firms, maybe on reflection, this wasn't such a bad idea after all. Our event coincided with the middle of the annual 'Greatest free show on earth', the fabulous Blackpool Illuminations.

One would be amazed at the large amount of coach parties that regularly visit this annual spectacular, coming from all corners of the British Isles. One now draws the obvious conclusion that this fact enabled us to 'cash in' on this spectacle which, in turn helped to swell the ranks of spectators considerably.

One final comment on this part of our activities is that our publicity colleague was so pre-occupied with catering for our needs in the few weeks prior to the event, that his own customers must have been relegated, albeit temporarily, to secondary consideration, which can't have been very good business.

One further side line we considered pursuing although regrettably it did not materialise, was that round about this time, the eagerly awaited 'Battle of Britain' film was being premiered in all the major cities throughout the country. Consequently, one of our club members had the brilliant idea of trying to obtain a copy of this film, to be shown at a midnight matinee at the local Odeon. It was thought that this would be a fitting prelude to our display on the morrow and swell our charity coffers into the bargain, by arranging tickets to be sold prior to the performance. Blackpool's Illuminations chief, responsible for the annual spectacular, another of our distinguished members, tried his utmost to bring about this extra publicity stunt but I'm afraid, to no avail. One can perceive that there was a lack of imaginative thinking in trying to spread the 'Gospel'.

The stage has now been reached whereby all the ground work has been thoroughly discussed in detail and all foreseeable snags have been resolved during the course of the past weeks and months.

All that remained, was to put the whole thing together and see whether we had done our homework properly by fitting the bits and pieces together in such a manner that the Air Display would not flop due to poor foundations. The time we allowed ourselves for this final build up, before the big day, was from the Monday prior to the 18th October right through to the 18th itself. I don't think John or myself will ever forget that week. It was to prove one of the most hectic we had ever endured. In fact on more than one occasion, we wondered if we hadn't taken leave of our senses, let alone leave in the other sense, to tackle the task.

Before proceeding further, I wish to record comments made by my colleague two weeks before the event which admirably summarises the stage of the exercise we had reached by that point in time. I quote: -

"At the time of writing there are just two weeks to go to what looks like being the largest Air Display ever held at Blackpool. All arrangements are now complete and the committee is concentrating on final details, which can only be carried out in the days prior to the event. The publicity for the event has stated that there will be the largest display of post war aircraft ever seen in the North of England. This statement certainly looks justified as to date we have a Boeing 737 of Britannia Airways, a Dart Herald of BUIA along with two others from Autair Limited, a Dakota of Air Ulster (in actual fact the last three aircraft were withdrawn at the last moment- authors comments) and an RAF Hercules and Andover. In addition to these large aircraft there will be the famous Hurricane and Spitfire which are being flown in from the RAF Battle of Britain flight at Coltishall. Also on the military side will be a BAC Strikemaster, a new aircraft which is just going into service and this will be surrounded by a display of armaments. Vertical take-off will be represented by three helicopters and in addition there will be numerous Business Executive and Light Aircraft: in all approximately 30 to 40 aircraft for the public to walk round.

The display itself commences at 2.00pm and as a novel idea, it is being opened and closed with a parachute display, opened by the local amateur club 'The Black Knights' and closed by the professionals, the RAF 'Falcons' free fall team. The hours between will be packed with continuous flying culminating in the display by the RAF Red Arrows; there is no doubt that this team, composed of nine Folland Gnat trainers from the RAF Central Flying School at Little Rissington, is the finest display team in the world and must be seen to be believed".

Six Days to Success- the Final Preparation

These six days were entirely devoted to implementing each and every aspect of the domestic arrangements which are a vital part of any outdoor event. When one hopes to attract the public in large numbers, their needs had to be well satisfied if we were going to make a good impression. Who knows, one might wish to repeat the exercise at some future date and the old saying" First impressions are the one's that count" is very much a truism.

The best way I can relate as to what took place during this final preparation period is to refer to my diary and give a brief account of our daily itinerary as follows: -

Monday 13th October- Crowd barrier and Public address system personnel and paraphernalia arrive on site to commence erection of poles, stalls, laying out wires etc. First Aid and Lost Children's' tent erected. Telephoned Hawker Siddeley concerning possibility of their representative aircraft, the HS 125 and WW2 Mosquito participating. Phone call from BAC Warton to finalise details re: their representation. Finalise guest list for President's tent and evening reception. Distribute Airport employee's complimentary tickets. Arrange accessibility for car/coach and pedestrian entrances. Arrange with appropriate Corporation Department clearing litter etc after the "do". Advised by local Evening paper management of erection of advertising signs in immediate vicinity of the Airport.

Tuesday 14th October – Continue supervision of crowd barriers and PA system. Concorde model, in crate, arrives on Queen Mary trailer for unpacking and display on allocated site. Confirmation of BAC's static Jet Provost hangarage, both before and after the display. Phone call from Chief Test Pilot Chester (Hawker Siddeley) regretting withdrawal of Mosquito due to unserviceability. Two phone calls from RAF Bourton-on-the-Water regarding fuelling arrangements for the Red Arrows. Phone call advising withdrawal of Lightning Aircraft due to unserviceability. Phone call from RAF Abingdon requesting Hotel Accommodation and other queries concerning the 'Falcons' parachute team. Further phone call from Hawker Siddeley advising of withdrawal of HS 125, at this rate we'll have nothing left! President's tent arrived for erection. Ascertain from Airport Director latest permissible deadline to close those portions of runways and taxiways that can be closed, to continue erection of crowd barrier and PA system. At this point it is well to remember that whilst all this activity was going on, the normal every day activity on the Airport had to continue unhindered which I'm sure did not go down too well with the resident employees, and operators, dependent upon the Airport for their livelihood; but nevertheless we managed somehow.

Wednesday 15th October- Crowd barrier and PA system personnel still hard at it- the airport is rapidly taking on a carnival atmosphere. The RNLI, one of the few non-aviation static display items, arrives for suitable siting. Advised by RAF that a Hercules aircraft will replace the Lightning in the display itself, things are looking brighter! Spoke too soon, 'Gold Leaf' Zlin withdrawn but being replaced by another Zlin at a cost of £100. Beagle Pup withdrawn- here we go again! Corporation Cleansing Department shown mobile toilet sites for servicing; subsequently withdrawn due to industrial action, can't win. Imagine the state of the toilets after thousands have paid their respects! List of Rotary Clubs members given to one of the resident Airport clubs who have kindly offered their premises as a vantage point and communal gathering place.

Thursday 16th October – Crowd barrier and PA system nearing completion. Numerous phone calls, both outgoing and incoming. By this time my office phone is becoming red hot. I must be involving the club in considerable expense, thank god it won't be coming out of my pocket! Personal copy of the Official souvenir Programme to hand – looks quite impressive – our printing member has done us proud.

Friday 17th October – The last hectic day of preparation. Thank goodness it's all over bar the shouting. By evening everything is in its appointed place and the Airport appears all set for the morrow. The catering marquees arrive and are set up. Last minute panic; none of the marquees are situated anywhere near mains water supplies; fortunately the Airport Fire service comes to the rescue and prevents a lot of 'red faces'. Incidentally this last item is just one of the errors on our part which could have let us down in no uncertain manner but for the quick thinking of certain individuals. Most of the remaining static items have by now arrived, plus the odd flying display participant giving, as I have said, a kind of carnival atmosphere. By the time we were virtually on our knees and there was still the evening 'Commentators briefing booze-up' to contend with. On reflection, a fitting finale to our efforts throughout the previous days.

Having just about reached the zenith of our original Air Display idea and, before winding up this narrative to complete the saga, perhaps a preview of the actual flying programme itself, plus the odd descriptive static item, is appropriate in order to indicate how the pinnacle of our mountainous effort resolved itself into a spectacle that the crowd thoroughly enjoyed.

'D' Day

Right up to the morning itself we had been enjoying an Indian summer. I awoke to what appeared at first light a continuation of this particular weather phenomenon, what a relief. Towards midday there was a temporary revision, which caused our pulses to quicken and the adrenaline to flow that bit faster. Throughout the morning of the eighteenth, all manner of last minute details and queries had to be dealt with and resolved long before we were able to open the 'flood gates' to the public.

The weather did continue sunny, but haze reduced the visibility somewhat which didn't augur too well for the flying display itself. I might add too that it was much colder than of late. However as I said at the beginning of this story, all in all our old adversary did us proud. I think the best way to summarise what transpired on that all-important day is to once again quote from an article my colleague subsequently wrote for the monthly club bulletin. In my opinion, his remarks are a fitting finale to our efforts.

'That morning I arrived at the Airport at 7.00am knowing that the type of weather we had been experiencing for the past couple of days would prevail, i.e. clear skies, moderate winds and poor visibility – not the ideal weather for an Air Display, but not an impossibility. The first two to three hours were frustrating and only too well do I remember being told that, due to the weather conditions elsewhere, the Spitfire and Hurricane would not be able to display. Then that the R.A.F. informed us that due to technical reasons the Lighting would not be available. Mr Simon Ames of the Royal Aero Club was, at this time, hard at work re-organising the form of display and assuring both John and I that successful displays had been held with many fewer participants, and under worse weather conditions, a real tonic to both of us, whether the facts were true or false.

My next memory is the arrival of our first display aircraft, the R.A.F. Hercules which had to overshoot from its first approach and was then brought in on radar, what weather.

Half an hour later, my day was made with the arrival in their usual inimitable way, of the Red Arrows, who were going to prove to be the makings of the display. From now until just after lunch, there were so many things happening that I have no particular memory. It was not until the display was well under way that I took time off to climb on to the roof of the control tower and look out on to the crowds and hear the Police Chief estimate the numbers at around 30,000 and to realise that weather or no weather, our efforts had proved a success.

Lastly, I remember certain club members checking the cash and realising that we had surpassed all expectations as to the money we had hoped to make. Finally and probably the most important memory of all, the simple fact that over 50% of the members of the club had turned out, supported us and physically worked from mid morning to early evening, what a credit to a Rotary Club'.

Conclusion

Not long after the conclusion of the display, darkness fell upon us fairly quickly and it was only now that we felt we could relax and enjoy the evenings shindig. However, before getting down to the serious business of wining and dining, various club officials and others made the most complimentary remarks to those assembled, most embarrassing!

Before summarising the final act in this drama, we weren't, as yet, completely finished with our efforts. There was the clearing up operation to be completed after any large public spectacle. This started immediately upon conclusion of the display, even before the crowds had finally dispersed, and continued for a number of days afterwards until finally the Airport returned to 'sanity' and we could relax and look back with pride on what we had achieved.

There is very little else one can say that has not already been said except that the fruits of our labours had attracted a crowd of approximately 32,000 which by any standards, bearing in mind the time of year, was exceptional, and £3000 was raised for charity. I believe this was the largest amount the club had ever raised on any one particular project in its entire history. When one considers that we had started off as complete amateurs, we were not unnaturally pleased with ourselves. One hopes that our heads did not swell in the process!

This is intentionally a relatively brief account of how an Air Display is organised. Were I to record each and every facet of this exercise, it might become a little unwieldy and consequently boring to the reader. If on the other hand this story contains some interesting facts concerning this form of entertainment then, having put pen to paper, Iwill rest content.

The next page contains our final balance sheet, which may be of interest to whosoever might contemplate undertaking a similar project.

Balance Sheet

Income	£
Receipts	6042.00
Prog Adverts	288.00
Expenditure	**£**
Hire of Marquees	70.00
Hotel Accommodation	300.00
Insurance	691.00
PA System Equipment Hire	200.00
Ambulances	11.00
R.A.F. Expenses	63.00
Hire of Advertising Banner	15.00
Display Signs	30.00
Printing and Advertising	433.00
Charter Aircraft (Commentator)	88.00
Posters and Bill Posting	189.00
Site Preparation	202.00
Catering	321.00
Programme Printing	491.00
Northern Aircraft Preservations Society	26.00
Incidentals	29.00
Royal Aero Club	131.00
Hire of Mobile Toilets	60.00
Displays on Brebs etc	46.00
	3406.00
Balance Carried Forward	2924.00
	6330.00

Epilogue

Three years later, a milestone in our Club's history had been reached namely its Golden Jubilee. The powers that be knew that a major event to celebrate this anniversary would be a fitting way to commemorate the club's half century of existence.

In our infinite wisdom the same two Johns volunteered to stage another Air Pageant. No doubt we were still flushed with the success of the previous occasion! Initially our suggestion was turned down due to the fact that our Secretary had discovered that a mistake had been made in the actual date of the club's foundation and therefore the half century was not due until the following year! The mix up had been caused by the fact that our club had been founded one year before its charter had been granted and therefore it was the latter date from which its Golden Jubilee should have been calculated. However, despite this enlightenment, our offer was subsequently accepted and so the rigmarole of 1969 was entered into with renewed enthusiasm. The format was similar to the previous Pageant except this time we decided to hold it earlier, rather than later in the season, the 13th May to be exact. We hoped the weather gods might look favourably upon us at that time of the year.

To cut a long story short and before appending the report which I was eventually asked to submit for the club archives, I must say that regrettably our second Air Pageant almost ended in financial disaster. I hasten to add, in mitigation, that the display itself was a considerable improvement over our first effort in as much that it was acclaimed by all and sundry as being a first class spectacle. Why was it a near financial disaster? Well, without making any excuses, the two basic reasons were as follows. First, our expenditure was doubled and the expected crowd numbers did not materialise. Second, the public, particularly the local inhabitants, had obviously got wise to the vulnerability of our Airport, from a spectating point of view. In other words the Airport's situation was such that large numbers of the public could view the spectacle just as well outside as it could inside the airfield. Human nature being what it is, only those of a more charitable nature chose to pay for their entertainment.

The up-shot of all this was that there were at least as many non-paying guests as there were of the paying variety. So consequently our 'gate' suffered considerably.

After weeks of anguish, our auditor informed us that we had made the princely sum of £27.00! A close shave to put it mildly. Small wonder that at the subsequent inquest, it was unanimously decided to call it a day as far as future Air Pageants were concerned.

My report, for what its worth is appended hereunder: -

"For my money (on second thoughts, perhaps it was as well that it wasn't!) the recent Air Pageant was a first class example of an Air Display, as they are commonly called. That is, a non stop display of professional pilots exercising their skills on mounts that varied from the largest aircraft in the show, the Vulcan, through to the incomparable Tipsy Nipper. Perhaps the last named should have been on Static display in the President's tent adjacent to the bar!

The Blackpool Illuminations are often described as being 'The greatest free show on earth'. I would now like to put on record that, this year at least, the Rotary Air Pageant merited equal status as no doubt it was enjoyed by as many people outside the Airport as by those who entered its precincts and paid for their entertainment. Whatever the pros and cons maybe, I for one am more than satisfied by the fact that, as our President so rightly said, this venture of ours was a perfect example of what the Rotary term 'Community Service' means. He also said that we, the members of the club, could be justly proud of the service we have given. The president's remarks and those from other notable sources, both within the club and from outside, make one feel that all the weeks and months of effort put into what is after all a mammoth undertaking by anybody's standards, particularly for a Rotary Club with limited resources, was not in vain. On that note, I rest content.

What about another Air Pageant some 'wag' may ask? I think my best answer to that one is to quote what some wit said to me shortly after the event. "To stop prying eyes, how about holding the next one under cover!" The mind boggles! Imagine the Red Arrows whistling about in a confined space like birds in an aviary. Perhaps the Rothmans with their more sedate Biplanes would be willing to oblige!

Of the pageant itself, we were indeed fortunate that we had not one, but three doses of this renowned R.A.F. Aerobatic team, in the form of their arrival prior to the event, their unique performance in the display itself, and during their finale, as it screamed across the aerodrome at nought feet. It was so low that one pilot had to 'kink' his machine to avoid hitting the tailplane of its supporting Hercules as the latter was waiting for take-off. Obviously, there was something more in those presentation tankards than met the eye!

Of the other participants, perhaps the Vulcan attracted the greatest interest due to its size and noise. This equally applied to the Phantom which, on the conclusion of its display, stood on its tail, engaged re-heat and then rocketed up to 20,000 feet in a matter of seconds. I could not do full justice to all the other display items in the limited space available, but suffice to say that they all, without exception, did their party piece admirably. The only real disappointment was not being able to see the Spitfire being put through its paces due to undercarriage trouble, although a few of us witnessed its potential when it gave a mini display on its arrival. Fortunately it landed back at its home base without mishap. I am also pleased to report that the precision of the 'Falcons' free fall parachute team negated the services of the three Blackpool Light Craft Club' boats standing by off-shore. We must ensure that the tide is well out or, alternatively, move the aerodrome further inland!

In conclusion, I would like to pay tribute to all the participants who appeared in our Pageant, The British Light Aviation Centre who programmed the display on our behalf, The Club President who took keen interest throughout the proceedings, John my co-organiser, a first class committee who took a lot of weight off my shoulders. Last, but by no means least, those members of the club, and other organisations, who gave up their spare time to help one way or another on the day which must surely prove that our motto 'Service above self' is no idle boast".

7   NORMAL OPERATIONS ARE RESUMED

Having related my involvement in the Rotary Air Display, I found the experience invaluable when I took to controlling one myself.

I subsequently took an active part in a couple of these events. At the risk of blowing my own trumpet, I have to say they were not as well attended as ours. This was not the fault of the organisers as they were up against circumstances beyond their control. Blackpool, due to its wide-open layout and, despite my previous remarks is not, after all, the ideal aerodrome for such events. Too many people can watch the spectacular from vantage points outside the airport. After all, the object of the exercise is to get the 'punters' IN to pay for their entertainment. Air Displays are costly things as witness my own experience in organising one. Where we, in Rotary, had the advantage was, that one of our members was the local Police Chief, who had the power to stop the public from viewing 'for free', by blocking off some of the outside airport thoroughfares.

What was it like to control such events? During the Display itself, it was relatively straightforward. There was always a display co-ordinator working alongside the controller. He programmed the individual events, timing being of the essence, and in some cases, I'm talking about seconds not minutes between display items.

We had to prohibit general aviation activity, apart from scheduled services and display participants. This didn't go down too well with our resident flying clubs, private owners, etc., but was reluctantly accepted as a safety measure. Just imagine the chaos that would reign, had we allowed circuits and bumps and other flying activity, to intermingle with an Air Display!

To set the scene then, normally the flying display axis is aligned along the main runway, the remaining ones being restricted to taxiing routes, and hard standings for static exhibits, such as Marquees, Trade Stands, Crowd Barriers, etc. I deliberately mention these facts as they have a direct bearing on the problems facing a display controller, as will be demonstrated shortly.

In the meantime, the interesting periods, from a controlling point of view, were prior to the start of the display and after it had finished. Due to all the bits and pieces dotted around the display site, some of which were placed alongside the display runway, one's view from the control tower became somewhat restricted. Hence my remarks earlier. This made life difficult for seeing landing and departing aircraft, tending to throw normal control procedures out of the window. You just kept your fingers crossed that nothing untoward happened.

After the conclusion of the display, controlling became even more hazardous. We were not helped in our work by those pilots, who were not stopping, started champing at the bit for a rapid return to their home bases. This was all very well but with one's ears being bombarded by impatient pilots demanding taxi and take off clearances, you literally took pot luck and hoped that when you issued instructions, bearing in mind that the aircraft you were talking to, was invariably hidden from view, that it was indeed the particular aircraft you had been in R/T contact with and not some other! Why there weren't any incidents during these particularly hectic periods, was more by luck then judgement.

Eventually sanity prevailed and with a big sigh of relief, normal operations resumed. On reflection, the very word sanity could be appropriate, in that one's state of mind could be called into question when having to cope with all this bedlam before, and after the event.

Having digressed, now its time I reverted to the role I was employed as, and attend to more immediate ATC matters. I have previously indicated how busy our locally based airline's route to the Isle of Man could get during the summer months. One of the problems we faced in ATC was due to the short sector flying times involved. Pilots were confronted with communicating with no less than three ATC agencies, they being ourselves, Preston Airways and Ronaldsway all within a time scale of only 25 minutes or so. Operationally this involved telephone calls to obtain airways clearance which, in turn had to be passed to the relevant aircraft by R/T, passing airborne times, obtaining release instructions from the two airports, etc. To alleviate all these telephone and R/T contact I, in conjunction with my opposite number at Ronaldsway, managed to persuade the authorities at Preston airways, to give us block clearances up to a specified height band, in which Ronaldsway and ourselves exercised control, without involving Preston. During peak periods this method of control worked very well and I know the pilots appreciated the reduction in their communication workload. For yours truly, having worked at Barton Hall, the experience gained there helped no end when we instituted this revised controlling procedure.

Now for a word about the type of airspace (i.e. Advisory Route [ADR]) our traffic was operating along. You will recall that aircraft are only controlled and separated from other aircraft whose pilots wished to participate in this limited ATC service. Here's the catch though; there is no mandatory requirement for aircraft flying along these routes to notify any ATC agency of its intentions. In other words, they were operating solely in the open Flight Information Region, outside controlled airspace. Consequently, any aircraft can transit or cross such airspace without the knowledge of the appropriate controlling authority. It was a bit of a GREY area in ATC operations. Not, in my opinion, a very satisfactory state of affairs but, I suppose better than no control at all.

To try and improve this situation, again I and my counterpart at Ronaldsway went one step further. We approached the overall hierarchy of ATC to see whether they would be prepared to up-grade this route to a seasonal airway status, so as to ensure full ATC protection to the passenger carrying aircraft flying this busy route. Alas, in their infinite wisdom, our Lords and Masters decided there was an insufficient movement rate to warrant implementing our proposal. At least no one could deny that we tried to regularise a situation that we considered was a rather indifferent control service. These being the days when radar coverage was minimal and therefore procedural control was the order of the day, with its inevitable restrictions. The introduction of radar at a later date, certainly eased the problem and due to the very nature of its capabilities, it considerably expedited the movement rate along this and similar routes. This facility certainly made the controller's job of keeping aircraft separated that much easier. Simply put, the radar controller could at least 'see' all his traffic, rather than having to rely upon pilot's reports, the accuracy of which had to be taken for granted. Radar also eased pilot's navigational problems in that it provided a constant monitoring service, checking upon an aircraft's flight path and, where necessary, re-routing aircraft to avoid bad weather, or give them a more expeditious routing.

In relation to Advisory Route (ADR) Traffic, it was particularly useful in that all aircraft under radar control, could be kept clear of unidentified or non-participating traffic thereby, to a certain degree, eliminating the GREY area of an ADR's limited control input of ATC operations.

What other aspects of my responsibilities did I get involved in?

First to come to mind were Non-State ATC Conferences. These took place once a year at different venues around the country. Watch-keeping duties permitting, I was required to attend these conferences.

The object of these seminars was to enable our licensing authority, the CAA, to update us on the latest rules and regulations affecting our profession and advise us of future operational changes that were in the pipe line. It also gave us SATCOs the opportunity to air our views and specify any problems we might wish to bring to their attention.

My contribution to these meetings tended to be a case of maintaining a 'listening watch' due to my reluctance to speak amongst strangers, although I did know some of my fellow SATCOs.

However there was one year when I did voice an opinion. So strongly did I feel about the issue in question, that I was prepared to stand up and be counted. The proposal I wished to submit centred around a night freight contract that had just been awarded to an operator at our airport, using just one aircraft. We didn't have the staff to man the airport twenty-four hours a day and therefore we in ATC could only offer one controller, operating without an assistant, to accommodate this contract. Our airport was not even promulgated as a twenty-four hour operation. To all intents and purposes we didn't exist outside our published hours of operation. Nevertheless, it was important that this night freighter not only departed from us but that it also returned to us, without incurring diversions or unnecessary delays to the operator.

Now to the crux of the matter as to why I submitted my proposal. Operationally controllers are not supposed to carry out two separate ATC functions at the same time, excepting the combined Aerodrome/Approach Control service already permitted by our rules of engagement. In our particular circumstances, because we realised the commercial importance to the airport of this night freighter, we wanted to ensure, as far as possible, that this aircraft would be able to return to us despite staff limitations and regardless of adverse weather. Our existing landing aids, apart from radar, being the NDB and VDF procedures, could not always guarantee a successful landing in poor weather conditions. So, I thought, why not offer our radar facility in addition to our normal Aerodrome/Approach service. It also occurred to me that if the operator had to divert on more than one occasion, due to the lack of a precision landing aide, then they might be tempted to look elsewhere for their business – an example, incidentally, of wearing my managerial hat in the interests of the airport's commercial operations. Management and I saw eye to eye on this one. Practically all the controller had to do was set up the radar well in advance of the returning aircraft's ETA, if the weather was suspect, inspect the runway (standard procedure) then, if it was necessary, go down to the radar room and conduct an approach. But I realised I could not enforce such procedures on those controllers who objected to my unorthodox methods! Well the consternation this 'modus operandi' of mine caused was almost unbelievable. It certainly stirred things up and even provoked heated arguments as to the validity of my arguments. This was NOT just a case of a 'cry in the wilderness', at the conference I was supported by one or two of my colleagues who faced similar situations at their own airports.

To cut a very long story short, the upshot of my proposal was that I was reminded that one of my responsibilities as a SATCO was to ensure the rules were obeyed. This attitude by our regulating authority, not withstanding my questioning their reasoning, was to me a perfect example of the time honoured phrase – "Rules are for the guidance of wise men and the obedience of fools" – how true! I still consider it was a perfectly safe way of operating and with tongue in cheek, I continued as before; without their knowledge of course!

On another tack, one of my unofficial roles as I saw it was, when opportunities arose, to promote the airport's assets by encouraging other operators to fly from and to us. In other words, try and drum up some extra business. One outlet we had was by way of the rapport we had established with our local aviation colleagues who had friends in the airline business or, indeed, were involved themselves. I had to accept, regrettably, that one of the problems with Blackpool was that we were in competition with two major airports down the road, namely Manchester and Liverpool. Amongst other factors in their favour, compared with Blackpool, was that they enjoyed the advantage of more staff, better navigational facilities, modern terminal complexes etc. The latter item, in our case, was more reminiscent of the wartime era. Our terminal building was nothing more than a collection of nissen huts joined together and tarted up with copious layers of paint, to represent an acceptable alternative. With our lack of essentials to attract would be customers, I am afraid we were on a losing wicket. Mores the pity as we enjoyed a good weather record and, apart from Blackpool Tower, we were obstruction free for miles around. Not many airports could match these two basic necessities for trouble free operations. All was not lost though, as we did have the odd diversion from some of the more prominent airlines.

Whilst on the same subject, another opportunity did arise for conjuring up business when I and those of my staff who were interested, were invited to a pilots/controllers forum organised by the BEA Silver Wings Club. This was in the days when the two British National Carriers were BOAC and BEA, before being merged into British Airways. The venue for this forum was held at Manchester's old airport, Barton aerodrome. During the proceedings and, despite my reluctance to speak up, I asked the assembled pilots what would persuade their companies to use our airport on a regular scheduled basis. Despite the fact that we had radar, their unanimous response was that, although they would welcome operating from our neck of the woods, the one facility we lacked was an Instrument Landing System (ILS). Unfortunately, at that period of the airport's history, money was tight. We simply could not afford such luxury, so our persuasive powers came to nothing. Some years later, 1982/83, when the financial climate had improved, the airport authority recognised this would be an essential investment if we were to keep up with the' Jones's'. I had long been an advocate of ILS but I didn't hold the purse strings to authorise such expenditure. The biggest advantage of ILS, compared with our radar, was that it was not subject to the vagaries of the weather. It was also a more precise landing aid and, I suspect, some pilots preferred this facility, rather than having to rely upon a controller's expertise in conducting radar approaches.

Other spin offs of the ILS system was its availability as a training facility, for enabling pilots to keep current their instrument ratings. Even RAF Hercules aircraft flew all the way from their base at Lyneham, Wiltshire to carry out practice instrument approaches, without landing, before returning to their base. It rapidly became a well used training facility and, as with other radio navigational training aids, its services had to be paid for, thereby swelling the airport coffers. You don't get something for nothing in this day and age!

What other schemes, of significance, did I get involved in? Liaison with Warton was one example. Due to their proximity, a lot of our traffic transited their airspace and, to a lesser extent, theirs infringed our circuit area. As a matter of interest, Warton's ATZ was larger than ours being, in shape, not unlike the 'Logo' of London Transport i.e. two half circles joined by parallelograms.

We already enjoyed a direct telephone link between the two ATC units, whereby co-ordination of our respective traffic situations could be effected. Nevertheless, it was decided that a more formal agreement, in writing, should be drawn up to safeguard against any misunder-standings that might arise from telephone communications. The prime objective was to establish which ATC unit was responsible for which traffic. I took it upon myself to submit a draft agreement and was pleasantly surprised when I showed my proposal to my opposite number at Warton for his comments. He could find little fault with what I had written and, on that basis, we implemented the agreed procedures,

Despite my reservations on administrative matters, and what they entailed, at least I had proved to myself that I was capable of formulating official policy, when I had to. In a sense, this document ensured that our 'backs were covered' in the event of anything untoward happening, a 'belt and braces' syndrome.

Another scheme I had in mind was how to relieve the congestion on the one combined Approach and Aerodrome R/T frequency which we had to operate. I was aware that some concern had been expressed by, in particular, our airline pilots, as to the effectiveness of the Approach control part of our operations, due to this R/T congestion. By that I mean that pilots were sometimes unable to make their appropriate calls to us and on occasions controllers could not always respond or warn them that they could be entering a busy circuit area. In other words, with the variety of traffic we had to contend with, both IFR and VFR, the two-combined ATC functions we were performing should, ideally, be separated. That is an Approach Control for IFR traffic and Aerodrome Control for VFR traffic, as is the case at larger airports. But, we were up against minimum staffing levels. As an interim measure and on the then infrequent occasions we had surplus controllers on duty at any one time, it occurred to me that using the radar frequency, when not required for talk-downs, might be a way out of this dilemma. We tried out a scheme whereby two controllers could operate the two frequencies and, sitting side by side, could effectively co-ordinate their respective control functions, as though they were separate ones. It certainly cut down the R/T chatter and improved the service we could offer, particularly for airline and other IFR traffic. VFR circuit details largely operated on the 'see and be seen' scenario and, not withstanding ATC were largely responsible for keeping themselves out of the way of IFR, and other aircraft in their vicinity.

When we were able to implement this improved measure of control, it was much appreciated, in particular by our airline 'boys'. At the same time it reduced the individual controller's workload. Regrettably it proved to be a short lived experiment, entirely due to our staffing situation.

Let me describe an activity that was beginning to increase in frequency. I refer to helicopters that, although already a familiar scene at the airport would shortly be increased in numbers even further. This was generated by a major helicopter operator whose activities will be outlined shortly. The first inkling we had of what was proposed was the construction of a separate helicopter complex, adjacent to the present main terminal building. More significantly, this venture into a major helicopter business could not have happened at a more fortuitous time in the life of the airport, as witness what happened next.

Our resident airline complete with their large maintenance hangar and engineering staff had recently 'upped sticks' and left for pastures new. I won't go into the reasons why this happened but, suffice to say, such was the blow to the airport's business interests, that a big question mark hung over the airport's future. Possible closure was even mentioned. Thanks, to what follows, our 'bacon' was saved. We were back in business and lived to fight another day.

By the way, our late lamented commercial operator was rapidly replaced by another airline that wished to cash in on the lucrative Isle of Man run.

Now to the circumstances that brought about this change in the airport's fortunes. Gas exploration work had been going on for some time in the Irish Sea between Blackpool and the Isle of Man. The upshot of this was that a gas field had been discovered 20 miles off-shore from us. More to the point and of considerable benefit to our future well being was the amount of gas found lying beneath the seabed. Enough in quantity to supply our part of the United Kingdom for the next 40 years, some find!

Because of this discovery and the fact that gas rigs are served mainly by helicopters, our airport was chosen as the main helicopter base for this operation. Once full production had started and to cope with the amount of gas on tap, four rigs were positioned off-shore to pump the stuff ashore at Heysham. The airport's role in supporting the helicopter operator, Bond Helicopters, was to assist them to maintain a scheduled service in transporting rig crews to and fro, plus other ancillary duties. In addition to this daily routine we were required to provide a nightly emergency service to cover, when needed, such things as casualty evacuation (known as CASEVAC). The only section on the airport affected by this requirement was ours so despite limited staff we managed to organise a system whereby one controller, in rotation, was rostered on a call-out basis. Fortunately our services were rarely required.

What was it like to control helicopters?

In a nutshell, quite simple really, due to their 'peculiar' flying characteristics, compared with conventional flying machines. If anything, from a controlling angle, our task was made easier by the fact that they could be instructed to hover, climb or descend vertically, in addition to 'behaving' normally. To put it another way, they could be slotted into any traffic pattern, without hindrance to others.

The type of helicopter's used by Bond's didn't even need a runway; at least not in the early stages of their operations. Any grass area was sufficient for their needs. In actual fact, two designated grass areas were already in place in order to give a measure of lateral separation from runways. These areas were identified by two large white crosses and were used not only by Bonds, but other helicopters as well. In fact these areas were in use long before the 'gas helicopters' arrived on the scene. Additionally, for the benefit of Bonds, we instituted a novel idea, which enabled the rig'boys' to depart and land nearer their own terminal complex, which was not far from the control tower. We used our building as a separation yardstick, in the following way. Depending upon the wind direction we instructed the helicopters to, say, take-off west side of tower, and land east side and vice versa. This method of controlling kept them even further away from all runways, yet another 'keeping aircraft' apart problem solved..

As these machines were all flown by professionals it made no difference to the way we handled them. Most of the rig flights, during daylight hours, were conducted under VFR, due to their short elapsed flying times and they flew low level to and from the rigs. Once they were clear of our Air Traffic Zone they changed frequency to Warton, who monitored their flights using their surveillance radar. Within our circuit area they were treated like all other aircraft, with the added bonus to us in ATC that, due their manoeuvrability, they were easier to slot in amongst conventional aircraft. Come to think of it, wouldn't our job be easy if ALL aircraft could 'gyrate' the way helicopters do?

If the weather precluded VFR flights for inbound helicopters from the rigs, the pilots carried out instrument approaches in exactly the same way as conventional aircraft, with the advantage to us in ATC that we could reduce the time scale between landings by virtue of the fact that these machines, unlike fixed wing ones, could immediately vacate the runway after landing, whereas the latter type of aircraft had to complete their landing run before the runway was clear for the next customer.

Before concluding this part of our operations I was once invited to go on a sortie to the rigs. Although you will recall that despite my previous aircrew experience, I developed a phobia about flying, I welcomed this invitation as I knew it would only be a low level sortie; my phobia related to high level flying, being I suppose a form of vertigo. This trip was certainly an eye opener. For instance, as we approached each rig the landing platform, jutting out one side of the rig, appeared to be no bigger than a postage stamp. One has to hand it to these helicopter pilots and the skills they have to acquire in landing and taking off from such small places. Just to make life a bit more interesting the jutting out platforms appeared to have no visible means of support in their construction! I thought to myself, there is an awful lot of sea to fall into if the pilot misjudged his approach! Fortunately, to my knowledge, nothing like that ever happened.

Another aspect in our profession, that one cannot ignore, is in the realm of training. In fact, I contend, that one never really stops learning in any profession you care to name.

For instance, whenever a new controller joined us he had to undergo a period of in house training, a subject I have already dealt with. Pete was the obvious choice for the role of Training Officer, as I am one of those persons who dislike monitoring other people's performance: I'd rather do the job myself. Having said that, I realised I couldn't completely disassociate myself from this essential task. After all, being the boss, I was ultimately responsible for the effectiveness of the training programme Pete had devised. Also it was my responsibility to alert the CAA Inspectorate when our u/t controllers were ready for validation.

About half way through my term of office, the CAA introduced annual competency checks for all non-state controllers, irrespective of who they were employed by. SATCO's were no exception. As I was more or less permanently 'glued' to the control desk, at least I was current with the ever changing rules and regulations and so, found these no hardship. I only ever failed once and this was after I had reached the magical three score years and ten age barrier. Having dealt with this part of my life, I'll say no more on that subject.

Like some other ATC units, we did have a scheme whereby those of our assistants who showed potential, were considered for controller training. Amongst other considerations we looked upon this idea as a form of insurance policy to guard against the times when controllers left our employ and sometimes the difficulty in recruiting qualified replacements. The controller market, like the pilot's one, had its peaks and troughs in the employment availability stakes. That's why we thought it seemed a sensible idea to have ready made controllers, on the spot, who could slot in at a moments notice.

I had two such characters that ultimately obtained their licences. All credit to them when one considers that they had to study for their written examinations, without the benefit of attending a specialised course as I, and most of my colleagues had done. The practical part of their training was conducted in the control tower, supervised by whoever was controlling at the time. One of these gentlemen, Mike by name, actually performed solo controlling duties throughout one particularly busy season. However, much to my and everyone's surprise, at the end of the day, he found the responsibility too much. Consequently he requested re-instatement in his original ATC position. A great pity, as he was more than competent in both roles. One can only push such persons so far, safety being the overriding factor. Therefore an individuals reluctance to perform a task he/she feels ill at ease with, cannot be ignored.

The other gentlemen, Harry by name, ultimately did him a lot of good. Although he didn't do any controlling with us, the last I heard of him was that he had been appointed SATCO of the North Sea Rigs helicopter operations. Such schemes as ours obviously paid dividends.

We also got involved in RAF controllers on pre-release training, prior to them entering the civilian ATC service.

To sum up then, one cannot ignore such intrusions into one's livelihood. At least, being involved in training other personnel, we kept ourselves current in all aspects of ATC, which, I'm sure, outweighed any misgivings we may have felt in thinking our training days were over.

Later on in my career, after I returned to the world of ATC, following my initial retirement, a privately owned helicopter school, in addition to Bond's operations was set up. The point I am trying to make was the inescapable fact that, what with increasing club activity, scheduled flights etc., controlling became even more involved. For example, we were now mixing helicopters, more often than not, being flown by trainee pilots, with similar category pilots of fixed wing aircraft; and all to be dovetailed into the mainstream of our operations. One thing though that made our life that little bit easier was that our helicopters i.e. the school ones, carried out their circuit activity in the opposite direction to the fixed wing type. The only time they appeared together was when they were on final approach but, even then, whilst the fixed wing's landed on the runway, the choppers landed on the grass adjacent the runway; yet another form of separation.

It will not be hard to imagine that, at times, we were confronted with some very interesting situations, testing one's controlling expertise. A challenging profession if you like that sort of life!

One feature of an airport's life that I haven't touched upon so far, are the inevitable accidents and incidents that occur, some of which tragically are fatal. During my whole time at Blackpool, we only had one major 'prang' involving more than one fatality. There were other accidents, mainly in the light aircraft category which, in some cases, the pilot was fatally wounded. Amazingly though, when one considers the amount of traffic we handled, our safety record was remarkably free from such unwelcome occurrences. In fact, some of the non-fatal, injury free incidents witnessed by others, and myself were most comical in their outcome, as I will try and illustrate later.

Safety Record

As the only major accident that occurred during my entire time at Blackpool, referred to on the previous page, the circumstances that caused this tragedy are perhaps worth recording, as it hit the headlines.

The aircraft was a Hansa Jet, which failed to get airborne and ploughed into the holiday camp, situated beyond the upwind end of the main runway, which the jet was using for his take-off run.

It was subsequently discovered that the elevator locking pins, between the pilot's legs in the cockpit, had been left in. Fortunately for the holiday campers they were in the dining hall which was some distance from their chalets, where the jet crashed. Amazingly, out of six persons on board this aircraft, one survived. There were no holiday camp fatalities or injuries.

Although I was not on duty at the time, I happened to be in my back garden idly watching this aircraft when, all of a sudden, there was a marked reduction in engine noise and instinctively I knew it was in trouble. Sure enough, seconds after it disappeared from view there was a loud explosion followed by a huge pall of black smoke.

Being the SATCO, albeit I was not on duty, my conscience dictated my presence might be required in the control tower, as, no doubt, the staff on duty would have their hands full in coping with the accident. I dashed over to relieve the controller, so that he could concentrate on organising the emergency services. It happened to be Pete, who was rapidly gaining a reputation as an accident-prone controller.

Inevitably there were a number of other accidents and incidents resulting in the odd fatality. In the non-fatal area of incidents, there were a number of bent aircraft, occasioned by student pilots, which was hardly surprising in the numbers involved.

All I can say is that, of those airports that submitted movement and safety statistics we were remarkably free of 'dramas'. Of interest, referring to the number of movements statistic, we almost up-staged London Heathrow on occasions despite not being a 24-hour operation.

Of the only two other fatalities that occurred, the irony was that they involved two of the resident Club Proprietors, who also happened to be the Chief Flying Instructors. The first one was a gentleman who, having survived the war as a Wellington bomber test pilot, died of his injuries in an avoidable Auster prang. The other gentleman, apart from being the flying club owner, was also an Hotelier. His accident in a

Beagle Pup was caused by mechanical failure as he was about to land. The two eldest sons of these gentlemen took over the reigns of their father's clubs becoming CFI's in their own right. Both clubs are still going strong.

On a more pleasant note, the following incidents and occurrences will, I like to think, illustrate that there is sometimes a humorous, even comical side to what, but for the grace of god, could have ended in disaster.

An unusual incident was the occasion when our departing Airport Director, on his last evening at Blackpool, before taking up a similar post at Manchester, decided to inspect the recently installed approach lighting on one end of the main runway. For this purpose he hired a club Cessna aircraft, he was an ex-war time Mosquito pilot complete with DFC, to carry out his inspection. For some reason or other he undershot the runway and ended up on the ground with a rather bent aircraft. He was pulled clear of his machine by three young schoolboys, who happened to be in the vicinity. Apart from the odd bruises, he was none the worse for wear. An inauspicious start to a new high profile job!

I also recall the following incident. An inbound scheduled Handley Page Herald flight, piloted by an old colleague, John Woodward, had his nose-wheel stuck in the UP position. Such was his handling of his aircraft, and subsequent landing, that his performance was photographed by a member of the aircraft's manufacturer, who just happened to be at the airport when this drama was enacted. The photographer's input was subsequently shown to interested parties as an example of how to cope with such a situation; a copybook illustration.

The next scenario I thought rather novel. Captain Lech, a former Polish Fighter Pilot, was one of the local airline skippers, a gentleman I had had the privilege of flying with during my civilian-flying career. He was considered by all his colleagues to be one of the most natural and gifted pilots around. Poles, like Italians, seem to have this reputation as pilots. Anyway, on this occasion there was literally a howling gale blowing along the subsidiary main runway. Lech was piloting a Bristol Freighter (B.170) and rather than taxi along the normal route which could have been tricky in gale force winds, he decided to take a short cut and line his aircraft into wind on the upwind part of the runway and let the elements blow him back to the take-off point. How he steered the aircraft going backwards I have no idea. I couldn't believe my eyes when I discovered what he was up to!

On another occasion the same pilot, inbound to land in a Dakota with one engine out, chopped the other one before touchdown, plonking his aircraft onto the runway in a 'dead stick' manner, no doubt thinking of the days when he landed his fighter in similar circumstances. In both incidents, he had a full complement of passengers. How to master flying machines!

On a similar theme, I once saw the following. Three Hercules aircraft with their powerful engines and paddle bladed propellers, lined up and took off on our shortest runway, about 1300 ft in length due, yet again, to a very strong wind, which precluded using another runway. What astonished me was that all three Hercules were airborne abeam the control tower, which is situated less than half the distance from the take off point, abeam this particular runway.

The wind factor influenced my actions on the following occasion. Bill Prest was piloting a passenger carrying twin engine De Havilland Otter, a high wing monoplane which, because of this configuration of the aircraft's structure, meant it could be difficult to manage in cross winds. This was the case in Bill's circumstances, as he was taxiing out for departure. His aircraft was rocking about quite alarmingly and at one period, it looked as though he could be blown over. He was obviously struggling to keep control, therefore, without hesitation I called out one of our fire tenders and positioned it behind Bill's machine, to act as a windbreak.

Even if I say it myself, an example of a controller using his loaf; our 'bible' does not cater for such situations.

Pete, who else, is my next source of anecdotes. Come to think of it, maybe he should have written my memoirs!

An Italian made Aeromachi aircraft, that was being used for pleasure flying, in which the engine had to be started by hand without the pilot on board, started taxiing of its own accord. This culminated in rather expensive noises as it shot across the apron into the side of a parked Vickers Viking aircraft, whose passengers were about to board!

The following incident was certainly comical. It was a home built aircraft whose pilot, like the Aeromachi episode, started the engine by swinging the propeller, resulting in a pilotless aircraft careering around uncomfortably close to the resident airline's hangar, before the owner could grab the wingtip to stop its gyrations! Needless to say, the hangar personnel dispersed very rapidly. Pete was so helpless with laughter that, having pressed the crash button, he couldn't tell the fire crew what the problem was!

What about the Dakota with first officer Bill Tillotson on board, who had a multiple bird strike on take off, smashing the windscreen completely? This resulted in him and his skipper carrying out a circuit covered in blood and gore before executing a safe landing.

Then there was the occasion when after taking off, Keith Whyham was told by the controller " I don't know how to tell you this Keith but your 'leg' has just fallen off" and his laconic reply, "Yes, I thought I felt a bump as we got airborne"!

The following is a rather harrowing story. It concerns a certain pilot from one of the resident flying clubs, who in his Cessna aircraft took off from Aberdeen, somehow set up the wrong VOR to fly to Newcastle and ended up half way across the North Sea When he discovered his error, the headwind was too strong and he ended up ditching and was lost.

The next story doesn't really qualify under the title of this part of my narrative nevertheless, I think it is worth recounting as it was a deliberate ploy to flout the law, with a happy ending. It comes under the heading Banner Towing. One of the clubs carried out this form of advertising, pioneered and flown by Brian Bateson. What he knew at the time but chose to ignore was that this type of aerial activity was illegal. On one particular occasion, the annual Conservative Party conference was being held at Blackpool. Its party leader, and then Prime Minister, Margaret Thatcher was presiding and, as it happened, during one of the conference days it was her birthday.

Brian being a staunch supporter of the conservatives decided to honour this event by flying up and down Blackpool's promenade, trailing a banner that read "Maggie, a happy birthday". When she saw this, it so delighted her that she instructed one of her aides to deliver a special 'thank you' message to Brian, obviously unaware he was breaking the law! Not long after, this archaic law was rescinded, poetic justice?

I was one of the more fortunate types of controller who seemed to escape being involved in such dramas. I did nevertheless, witness a few unusual aircraft contortions, mainly in the hands of inexperienced pilots, some of which were quite hilarious.

We did have our share of accidents to those aircraft inbound to us, or departing elsewhere, but none of them happened on our doorstep, so they became somebody else's responsibility.

Incidentally, I can only once remember being on duty when the dreaded words "MAYDAY, MAYDAY, MAYDAY" came over the radio. On this particular occasion, during a quietish spell, I took to practicing my golf swing. At the top of the backstroke, just as I was about to bring the club head down, those very word came over the loudspeaker. I was so taken back by this R/T call that my initial reaction was, what a peculiar call-sign, which bore no relation to what little traffic I had displayed on my Flight Progress board. Then the penny dropped and my reactions became instantaneous, as per my training in how to respond to such emergencies.

As it turned out, the aircraft in trouble, a home based twin engine machine that was returning to us from somewhere up North, was caused by finger trouble by the pilot. He sent his distress call when both his engines stopped, only to realise a short while later that he had forgotten to switch from the empty fuel tank to the full one.

Its situations like these that emphasise the 'need to know' philosophy that is all part and parcel of a controllers way of life.

Some of us, no doubt, will never experience such happenings. Its not so much a question of what one does in coping with unusual occurrences but, of equal, importance, having the background knowledge of how to deal with such situations. This aspect of our responsibilities is instilled into us during the course of our training.

A further example of our duties as controllers was to bear in mind the question of wake turbulence. A problem that was not fully understood previously. This part of our controlling expertise was partly brought about by an unfortunate, indeed tragic accident which occurred some years ago at Carlisle Airport.

A four engine Argosy type aircraft, on a take-off run, was closely pursued by a light aircraft, also taking off on the same runway. The wake turbulence mentioned above was believed to be responsible for causing the light aircraft to flip onto its back and crash, killing all the occupants. In other words, the turbulence from the departing Argosy was deemed a contributory factor.

Whether it was this incident, or a hazard that had been given some thought but not seriously considered, guidelines were introduced in our 'Bible' to try and negate this problem. This instruction resulted in introducing timed intervals between different types of aircraft, be they light, medium or heavy, both relative to take-off and landing configurations.

We as controllers, as in the case of aircraft separation standards, really needed to know the differing criteria like the backs of our hands rather than having to refer to the book every time such a situation arose. Possessing a mentally agile mind was a bonus. In fact, if one had a photographic memory of all the rules and regulations one's job became a lot easier.

To round off this part of our duties and subsequent 'modus operandi', we could not afford the luxury of office type 'Pending trays' which, I suppose, is stating the obvious. Instantaneous instructions on our behalf was, of necessity, the order of the day at all times.

One has to be a particular breed of person to accommodate our profession.

8 PEDESTAL OR PRINCIPLE?

A Career Decision – 1981

Little did I know it at the time but my days as the SATCO were numbered. What were the circumstances that resulted in my resignation as SATCO?

For sometime management had hinted that I should take on additional responsibility namely Assistant Director Operations (ADO). No doubt some SATCOs would welcome this additional status symbol, but for myself, this was a sphere of Civil Aviation Operations that I had little knowledge of and, quite frankly, was not particularly interested in. So I resisted such approaches. The more I resisted, the greater the pressure was put upon me to accept management's arguments in creating this post. Without going into all the ramifications that led to my resignation, I think it only fair to put my side of the argument as to why I refused to comply. I admit, up to date, I had had an uneasy relationship with management and I suspect they were trying to force my hand into accepting something they knew full well I wouldn't want.

Anyway back to the, matter in hand, my refusal followed the following arguments. For example, in the CAA Operations Officers require specialist training and are, consequently, recognised as a separate profession, compared to ATC. Major non-state airports do recognise this fact and create separate roles, to look after the two disciplines, namely SATCO and ADO positions. I do, however, accept that at smaller airports like ours, where staffing can be tight due to financial constraints, there is a case in favour of one person undertaking the combined roles, but in my circumstances, were I to accept this additional responsibility, I would be unable to do justice to both functions. I was quite content to look after ATC matters, rather than be 'Bogged' down in unfamiliar territory. I was also of the opinion that where airports did, of necessity, combine these two posts, one or other suffered in a commitment sense. As I was fully committed to controlling duties, there was no way I could accept what was proposed.

Furthermore, in defence of my role, purely as SATCO, what I wrote to management subsequently, should illustrate the reasons why I wouldn't play ball? I quote: -

"Since 1965 the total annual movements at the airport have nearly trebled. The total daily hours of opening have almost doubled to nearly 24 hours, whilst my controller staff has increased by only two, from six to eight including myself; and my assistant staff by one, from three to four. This despite the fact that the airport is listed as being the third busiest (on occasions) in the country, during the summer. As one controller at Blackpool is handling all aircraft movements at any given time, a situation that does not apply at any other major airport in the country. It will be readily understood that each controller's workload is consistently very high, mine being no different to the rest of my staff. It has, in fact, been proved that by comparing the number of movements, to the staff employed, our individual workload is double that of any major airport in Britain. The safety record of the airport is very good and of those accidents that have occurred, no blame has been attributed to my staff. The annual reports from the CAA examiners show that a high standard has been attained, and maintained, by my staff and myself. Complaints from airport users are very rare. The records will show that, up to the turn of these events, the turnover of staff has been low.

I rest my case. My resignation was accepted and, by request, I was retained as a watch-keeping controller.

Before signing off as SATCO, it would be remiss of me if I didn't mention, apart from those already mentioned, some of the characters of note who worked with me during my term in office.

An old flying R/O colleague of mine- Norman Piper- who, like me, had opted for ATC upon the demise of our flying trade, became one of my controllers, at my instigation. He was a dour character and, apart from his dress sense, being casual in the extreme, he had a unique filing system, which he carried about his person; that being bits and pieces of paper of all shapes and sizes, stuffed away in all his pockets. Apart from being friends of his family, I was glad to have him aboard as a reminder of times past we enjoyed in the flying game.

At one time, much to my surprise, three controllers joined us from Warton. I say surprised as I always thought they were on a better salary scale, and conditions of service number at Warton. Maybe they got fed up with constantly being at the beck and call of test pilots, a trait I'm told is very much prevalent at manufacturer airfields. There must also have been long periods when test flying didn't take place, which probably increased the boredom level of their livelihoods. They rapidly discovered though, that Blackpool was no easy number, which undoubtedly accounted for the fact that their stay with us was not that long. A case of ' the grass is not always greener on the other side'! Nevertheless, interesting types by the names of Harry Meddings, Jack Bettany and John Baker. Harry was an ex squadron leader, who had the misfortune of being shot down at the beginning of World War 2, spending the rest of the war as a POW. He had a pet hate in ATC, which centered around non-radio aircraft. In fact, one of the club proprietors, in the early days, was aware of Harry's distaste and deliberately wound him up by flying his aircraft non-radio despite most of his machines being radio equipped.

Jack was ex wartime aircrew; having been awarded the rare gallantry medal, the CGM, second only in valour to the VC. His penchant, not linked to work, was to try and inveigle colleagues into lunchtime 'booze' sessions in any local hostelry and then, en masse, return to his maisonette for his 'piece de resistance'. After more drinks at his homestead, he would invite his guests to climb out of the window and shin down the fire escape, sometimes with disastrous results! Avoiding Jack at lunchtime became quite an art!

John, like Pete, was a natural at the job, despite neither of them having had aircrew experience. He eventually left ATC and became a successful Publican in Preston. Towards the end of my reign as SATCO, two elderly controllers were foisted upon me, despite my reservations as to their ability to cope with the level of activity we were faced with. I had nothing personal against these gentlemen but I did wonder if they were aware of what they were letting themselves in for. ATC at a place like Blackpool was, in my opinion, becoming more of a youngish person's type of profession. Admittedly, I was no spring chicken but at least I had the advantage of several years' experience in a busy working environment. Jeff had spent most of his ATC days with the Americans who, from all accounts, had the reputation of being hard taskmasters. John, on the other hand, had had a varied background, mainly on RAF stations where ATC was manned by civilian personnel. Despite my reservations, they both validated and became welcome members of the team.

A word or two about these two. John like the previous eccentrics I have mentioned, was quite a character. He was a big man in stature and personality. His controlling instructions were punctuated by the following gems of R/T phraseology, such as greeting colleagues and aircraft alike, by "How the devil are you, you silly little bastard". Another gem was when, on a particular day, fog covered the airfield, but the coast was clear. The continued bleating of one pilot who kept saying he could see the beach but not the runway, prompted the response from John "Well land on the bloody beach then"!

Apart from ATC, his major interest was Militaria and he would often appear with an assortment of bits off tanks, submarines, aircraft and vehicles, together with a veritable arsenal of weapons, including lugers, daggers etc. He also dressed the part as well and you could often be in the presence of Rommel or Goering! Indeed, during the Falklands conflict he dressed as an Argentinean pilot, donning a wig, false moustache and sunglasses and went into our Met. Office where he enquired of a startled forecaster, if he could obtain an 'actual' weather report for Goose Green!

Like Jacko and Indian Ron, he liked his food. It was not unusual for him to disappear to the kitchen and return a little later with a "light snack' which consisted of usually a whole packet of sausages, six eggs and a tin of baked beans, fried slices, mushrooms etc. Well as I said, he had a big frame to fill being 6 feet 4 inches tall and all of 16 stone.

Jeff, on the other hand, was more of a straightforward kind of guy. He, in his off duty days, quite often lectured at the flying clubs on Navigation and Meteorology, at which he was a past master, having been an ex RAF Navigator.

Ironically Jeff started off as my deputy and upon my resignation, took over the SATCO reigns in place of Pete who had departed elsewhere as a result of the SATCO/ADO drama recently enacted, in which he supported my battle with management

Apropos the following observation, I used to have a little smile to myself when I thought of some of the controllers I was responsible for. Most of them were ex Officers in the services and here I was a mere ex senior NCO in charge of this lot. As far as I know, this wasn't held against me!

My philosophy in man management, particularly with controllers, was that they were all professionals, who wouldn't welcome me telling them how to do the job, once they had validated. I cannot claim that all those characters who worked for me necessarily agreed with the way I wanted ATC at Blackpool to operate, but one way or another, I think they contributed to a reasonable ATC/Pilot relationship.

I like to think that I can look back on my 16 years as SATCO as being possibly the most interesting and rewarding part of my ATC career, enhanced by notable and varied characters that performed under my umbrella. Four other controllers of note are worth a mention, they being Nigel James, Pat Phrakun, Clive McKrell and Bob Womersley who, at varied times 'enjoyed' the delights of being involved in Blackpool's, some would say, unique area of ATC operations.

To sum up then, I make no apology for the time I have spent in my memoirs on the subject of 'characters' who injected, albeit in some case unwittingly, a sense of humor into our working environment. ATC, by its very nature is basically a serious profession, but as indicated, it does have its humorous side. Without this, none of us could stay in the business and at the same time cope with some of the stresses inherent in such an occupation.

POSTSCRIPT

I mentioned early on in my memoirs the problem of integrating IFR and VFR traffic and how we, as controllers, endeavoured to keep the varied mix of aircraft apart, both within, and in the vicinity of the limited airspace under our jurisdiction (The ATZ), in particular when it was busy.

As most of our controlling functions were concentrated within these areas, I omitted to describe one of the more obvious solutions in resolving potential conflicting situations. So, without further ado, let me put the record straight. Quite simply, it boiled down to a question of height separation, as shown by the following examples: -

1. Circuit details were restricted to 1000 feet.

2. Inbound IFR aircraft were kept at 1500 feet initially and, likewise, departures were kept at the same height until they were clear of the circuit area; circuit details were always kept clear of an outbound aircraft's track.

3. Aircraft rejoining from an off circuit detail or, inbound from elsewhere, were required to join overhead at 2000 feet.

Right away it can be seen that we had created a 500-foot buffer zone between the participants, be they in the circuit, joining or departing.

Problem solved or, at least parts of it.

Is it not said, that there are times when simple solutions to a problem, are more often than not, the most effective?

9   BACK TO SQUARE ONE – 1981/87

Some people tended to see me as more of a figurehead rather than a Manager of Air Traffic Services. Be that as it may, nevertheless I like to think that I had, with the help of my staff, contributed to improving the image and professionalism of ATC in the eyes of our customers. If that is the case, my 16 years as the boss had not been in vain. This new stage in my career was to continue for another 6 years. Surprisingly enough, my self imposed relegation to being an ordinary watch-keeping controller, turned out to be a much easier transitional period than I had imagined. It hadn't, until now, sunk in that during the preceding 16 years, apart from my controlling and managerial responsibilities, I had been virtually 'on-call' 24 hours a day, 7 days a week, 52 weeks a year. One drawback to living on top of the 'shop'.

The new found relief in only doing my rostered shifts, after which I could go home and forget about it till the next shift, was a huge weight off my shoulders. The gentleman, who had been my deputy, now took up the SATCO position and promptly nominated me as Training officer. I hadn't, after all, been entirely relieved of my former responsibilities! Jeff, my successor didn't have a very long innings in the hot seat, as he wasn't far off retiring age, added to which he developed medical problems, which terminated his career in ATC.

For some reason or other, after Jeff left, the SATCO post remained vacant for some considerable time, which created a sort of vacuum in our section. In other words, we were like a ship without a rudder. In some ways a rather pleasant situation in which we found ourselves. No 'Big Brother' to keep a beady eye upon us. Is it not said, 'when the cats away the mice will play'! In a nutshell we were left to our own devices, unhampered by directives from above, which enabled us to enjoy a generally relaxed working environment, all within the letter of the law, of course! Whether the drama of late had any bearing on what follows I don't know but we detected a marked improvement in our relationship with management. A necessary ingredient in the overall workings of an airport.

In the absence of a SATCO to represent us in airport policy, whenever our views were sought, someone in ATC had to act as a spokesman. No prize for guessing that, due to my background, yours truly once again became involved. This time though, I took the precaution of enlisting another controller colleague, to assist me and safeguard against any repercussions that might arise, if there were differences of opinion between them and us. Nevertheless, one had to recognize that management did have overall authority to ensure their policies, in running the airport, were met. My new found freedom enabled me to further improve upon my controlling skills in all the infinitely varying ATC situations I would be confronted with. As I have said before, no two consecutive shifts, traffic wise, could be predicted as identical controlling patterns. To me, the variety of our profession made life interesting and satisfying, if one's controlling methods resulted in avoiding potentially hazardous situations. In this game, one really had to be on the ball. Admittedly, not all my colleagues shared my enthusiasm for this kind of ATC activity and, in due course, some of them elected to seek employment at less active airports. I can only conclude that I must have had a masochistic streak in my make up.

Due to continuing staffing problems, which never entirely ceased, we found ourselves short yet again. Maybe this was one of the reasons that management changed their tune in their attitude towards ATC and decided, as a matter of policy, to keep in with us. One of the ideas they introduced was to hold monthly meetings with all section heads. The outcome of which, by means of minutes recorded, were distributed to all airport employees, keeping them continuously in the picture of the fortunes and problems the airport faced. As we were only a small community, less than 65 employees all told, this proved to be a good PR exercise in keeping staff in the picture, a feature that had not been accorded such importance previously.

As regards ATC operations, the 'menu' was much the same as before. The clubs and private flying were as active as ever. Charter and executive flights were, if anything, on the increase and some of these were operated by foreign companies. All good business in the interests of the airport's well being.

Gliding operations had long since ceased, only to be replaced by increasing helicopter activity. Parachuting had also virtually become extinct although it was allowed during specific periods, mainly at weekends, early in the morning before the clubs, etc. stirred from their slumbers. Operationally they needed a clear airfield to carry out their jumps, so as not to get entangled with propeller driven aircraft wandering about. Why anyone wants to leap out of a perfectly serviceable aeroplane, is beyond me! Everyone to his or her chosen pastime I suppose.

Even non-radio aircraft were fast becoming an item of the past. The only time we had to resort to using the Aldis Lamp was on the rare occasions when aircraft developed radio problems, or when vintage aircraft, invariable without radio, paid us a visit. Now for a comment on how winter operations, in particular snow and ice, affected our livelihood. For starters, the onset of winter was a welcome break from a busy Spring and Summer schedule.

Because the airport was situated on the door-step of the Irish Sea, we were, relatively speaking, free from most typical winter weather conditions. In fact, I can only recall one occasion when, due to an unexpected heavy snowfall, we actually had to close the airport for a while, known in our profession as a SNOCLO condition, as our limited resources for snow clearance couldn't cope. On this particular day, due to the amount of snow that had fallen, I had difficulty in driving my car from the control tower to the airport exit a matter of a couple of hundred yards or so. How did we deal with these conditions? Initially when snow or ice formed, it was the controller's job to determine the snowfall depth on the runways and taxiways. To achieve this, would you believe, in the early days of my time at Blackpool, we used an ordinary Classroom ruler to measure the depth! Later on we were provided with a purpose made depth gauge, being a trifle more accurate in its readings. Then we had to decide the priorities upon which runway and taxiway should be cleared first. The physical side of snow clearance rested with our fire section. For their pains, quite apart from being qualified firemen, they were called upon to deal with all manner of jobs affecting the physical characteristics of the airport, snow-clearance being just one of them. Their equipment was rather basic, albeit they did have snowploughs of sorts but invariably they had to resort to the back-breaking shovel method of clearance. Considering they weren't blessed with more sophisticated equipment, enjoyed by larger airports, they coped pretty well. Ice was a different matter, which we experienced more of during frosty conditions, which were quite prevalent. The way we coped with this contaminant was quite novel. A product called Urea Prills was used, being nothing more than Pigs P*** converted into capsules which, when laid, rapidly melted the ice. Its only drawback was that it was no good on snow.

Another task we called upon the fire section to carry out was, to regularly wash down the control tower windows, using their powerful water jets, this being the only way salt accumulation from the sea, could be removed.

Having mentioned the fire section, it would be remiss of me not to mention those other sections, some of which we worked close with, others not so close, nevertheless, whatever their role, they formed an integral part of an airport's make-up. In my dealings with other sections, both as the SATCO, and as an ordinary watch-keeping controller, I like to think that I enjoyed a good working relationship.

The closest section we worked with was the radio department, as they provided us with the tools that enabled us to operate, in the first place. They being such items as R/T communication equipment i.e. transmitters and receivers, VDF, NDB and Radar Navigation aids, not forgetting the banks of tape recorders, installed in their workshops, which recorded all messages between us and aircraft and vice versa.

Amongst the personnel in this section, a couple of characters of note are, I think, worth a mention, if only to show that ATC did not necessarily commandeer the market in personalities.

The first one, Barry Edmondson, was an ex CAA technician. What he didn't know about radio and all things electronic, wasn't worth knowing. He was, in my opinion and others the finest technician we ever, or were likely to have. Unfortunately though, he was not a very fit person, having suffered a heart attack, crushed vertebrae and other afflictions, which, to a lesser person, would have crippled them. He never complained about his aches and pains. On the contrary, he was always cheerful despite being a walking medical disaster. Although younger than myself, he took early retirement at the same time as I did, no doubt due to his health.

The other character, Charlie Lancaster, also a first rate technician, had a deformity which affected his walking gait. He always appeared to walk to the left, hence his nickname 'Port drift Charlie'. I know one shouldn't laugh at other peoples misfortunes but it was comical to watch, not that he was aware of the 'title' we had given him! In the early days PBX and Teleprinters were housed next door to the Met. Office, in the control building. Later on they were moved to the Admin. Block as being more accessible to the airport tenants. The control tower, due to its remoteness from the terminal complex was not the best place for conducting day to day business. Now for a brief word on one of the Met: people with whom we regularly dealt. One in particular went by the name of Ken, whose enthusiasm for all things meteorological knew no bounds. He was extremely meticulous in keeping records up to date. One thing you didn't do though, unless you wanted an ear bashing, was to enquire after his health. If you did fall into this trap, you got half an hour of all his aches and pains, real and imaginary; and to think, so I was told, that he was once an athletic type! Another Met: character was a person by the name of Walter Smith (Smithy) who was the Met: chief when I first went to Blackpool. I mention him because of his knack of predicting very accurately the weather around our area. Officially he was not a qualified weather forecaster but such was his reputation on this score, that the local paper, The Evening Gazette, repeatedly featured his weather reports.

Now to the other sections. For example, the electricians, who looked after the airfield runway and taxiway lighting installations. They, in fact, came under the radio section umbrella.

The personnel we least had dealings with, unless you were a Section Head were, to use a common expression, the Admin. Wallahs. Their Supremo being the Airport Director, followed in descending order by his Deputy, Secretary, and office personnel who kept the wheels of administration well oiled. Without them, the airport could not function as a business enterprise.

Having given a brief outline of how the various sections were involved in airport operations we, meanwhile, in ATC continued to enjoy our leaderless freedom, knowing full well that this idyllic state of affairs could not last for ever. Sure enough, in the fullness of time, a suitable candidate was found and installed as our SATCO. He was a young man from Bristol Lulsgate Airport called Mike Parkes. He was one of those rare breeds who could do half a dozen jobs at once, no doubt helped by his acknowledged high I.Q. Just as well, as he undertook the dual role I had refused i.e. SATCO/ADO. His grasp of the not inconsiderable amount of matters that had to be dealt with, during the preceding period without a SATCO, he took in his stride. A very pleasant young man to be the leader of the pack.

I had cause to be grateful to Mike later on, when he re-instated me as one of his controllers, as will be revealed in the final pages of my MSS. My rapport with him was partly due to the fact that, I am one of those persons who seems to have more of an affinity with younger people, compared to those of my own generation.

During the latter part of the 1980's the government, in the course of its privatisation programme, turned their attention to airports, like ours, which were encouraged to shed their local government shackles and place themselves in the private ownership market. This change in ownership also affected the future of existing staff, not least myself, as I was not far off normal retirement age. Whilst these proposed changes were going through the motions, I was confronted with two alternative course of action I could take. Firstly, I could soldier on till normal retirement age (I was nearing 62 at the time) with the uncertainty of what the privatisation future held or, secondly, I could take early retirement, with incentives, that would be difficult to refuse. I elected for the second alternative, the advantage of which I will describe in a moment.

I must admit I didn't really feel like giving up a job I enjoyed, and still felt capable of doing, but circumstances, for the time being anyway, dictated otherwise.

Being a person with no particular hobbies, the thought of idling away my time for the rest of my natural, did not exactly appeal. As it happened, little did I know it at the time but this wasn't going to be the one and only occasion I would retire, more on that subject shortly.

By electing to accept my employer's terms of retirement, they did indeed do me proud. In addition to a generous gratuity, my reckonable pension service was extended to my normal retirement age, bearing in mind I still had three and a bit years to go. All in all, a very handsome termination of employment package, which I would have been a fool to refuse.

After 24 years spent controlling aircraft at what I call a very active airport, I can well remember my last shift. It was a typical Sunday morning and being late spring, it was busy. This didn't stop a colleague playing a trick on me, catching me completely unawares.

I had just cleared one of our schedules for take-off, bound for the I.O.M., intermingled with circuit details and other light aircraft activity when an 'American' voice called me up requesting transit, through our circuit of three Phantom jets, due any second. Because of the circuit activity and the recent airliner departure, I had my work cut out to clear these 'aircraft' through my airspace at such short notice. Needless to say, I never saw these jets! It wasn't till after they supposedly ' cleared' my area that I twigged that something untoward was going on. Even the departing schedule, who was still on my frequency, cast doubt about the 'traffic' situation presented to me. Sure enough, my colleague appeared in the control room beaming all over his face. Only then did I realise what he had been up to. Unbeknown to me, he had disappeared into the radar room, to pull this stunt. I had to give him his due, his American accent and typical Yankee R/T terminology took me completely by surprise, so authentic was his little game of make-believe. He should have been in the acting profession! To cap it all, again without my knowledge, someone had taped this whole episode. I still have the tape.

My departure from the control tower by car, after my last watch, was heralded by one of our fire engines, which I mistakenly thought, was going to give me a drenching for services rendered! It was only afterwards that I learnt they only wanted to mark my retirement with a watery archway, as a farewell gesture, nice thought and much appreciated.

When I had woken up to the fact that I had retired, the thought that I would no longer have to watch the clock, that I was free to do as I pleased, eased the pain of what I know a lot of people feel, initially, upon the end of their working life. One day employed, the next, on the scrap heap.

I was fortunate in working in a profession I enjoyed, unlike so many, who appear to spend their employment years in dreary occupations.

At least my long suffering and supportive wife who had spent a lifetime looking after a shift worker would no longer have to put up with irregular meal times, late nights and early mornings. Despite my reservations about retirement, I did manage to keep myself active, both physically and mentally.

By way of consolation and to celebrate my retirement I treated the family to two superb holidays. The first to Jersey with my wife's brother and his wife, the second to Newquay in Cornwall, this time just my family. Up to now, we had considered ourselves lucky if we managed one good holiday a year, an ideal way to start my life of leisure, or so I thought. Read on to what happened next!

10 SECOND TIME AROUND – 1989-1995

Eighteen months after retirement I found myself back in the world of ATC due to unexpected circumstances. I was still living by the airport and as I continued to socialise there I was tipped off that R.A.F. Woodvale, an aerodrome south of Southport, who operated a civil ATC unit were in urgent need of a part time controller and was I interested? I could not believe my ears as I was admittedly becoming increasingly disenchanted with retirement. I hasten to add that my disenchantment with my present existence had nothing to do with my home life. I just could not get used to the idea of not being actively employed.

To say I was interested in this heaven sent opportunity to re-install myself in my old profession would, to coin a phrase, be putting it mildly. One snag though I had let my controllers licence lapse (renewable annually by medical). If my prospective employer was prepared to pay for the renewal of my licence then I was theirs for the asking. My request was granted and after the usual formalities had been completed I found myself commuting backwards and forwards two or three times a week to my new 'playground'. The set-up at Woodvale was a curious mixture of R.A.F. and civil operations, the former being predominant.

As indicated, although it was an R.A.F. aerodrome, it was staffed mainly by civilians, for example, apart from ATC, there was a civilian fire service. Aesthetically speaking it was a very 'pretty' establishment, situated in a pleasant rural area. It was a typical service aerodrome with the standard three runways, and associated taxiway layout. My new habitat, the control tower was a standard R.A.F. watch office building, with a control room, which quite frankly, was more like a chicken coop, being very basic in its design!

The main types of aircraft flown were DH Chipmunks and Bulldogs. They were used principally for training University Air Squadron cadets, their instructors being R.A.F. officers seconded for that purpose

There was also a civilian flying club operating, in the main, Cessna and Cherokee aircraft. Despite it being a service aerodrome, civilian aircraft on a prior permission basis (PPO) were welcome. Most of the latter visitors came from my old ATC unit which if nothing else relieved any 'home sickness' I may have felt! The control tower console contained a layout that I had not come across before. Let me elaborate.

The visual presentation of aircraft details was totally different to what I had been used to. For example, the FPS format didn't exist, being replaced by what I subsequently learnt was a 'pin board' system. I had heard that some military aerodromes used this format but, to me, it was a new kind of aircraft presentation that I had to get used to. For example aircraft details were represented, literally, by large round headed pins containing very basic information, such as aircraft call-sign or, In the case of the University students, each student was allocated a three-digit number. The pin board was divided into separate compartments to indicate where each aircraft was, be it taxiing, taking off, landing, or flying away from the circuit area. The pins being placed on the board in their respective compartments. It took me sometime to get orientated with this pictorial presentation of one's traffic, particularly as I only appeared infrequently on duty. I cannot, in all honesty, say I was enamoured with this set-up. I preferred the civilian version of traffic presentation.

I also found that R.A.F. R/T communication procedures were different, adding to my initial controlling problems. A classic illustration of this happened to me at the first time I sat at the control desk. An inbound R.A.F. aircraft called me up with the word 'initials' whereupon I was tempted to say 'mine are JK what's yours'! Only when I asked my mentor what this term meant, was I informed that such calls are standard procedure for military aircraft wishing to join the circuit for landing. Maybe it was just as well I didn't yield to temptation, it would have been most embarrassing! Another aspect of military procedures I had to get used to, was the type of circuit their aircraft carry out, due mainly to the fact that the majority of university students, in training establishments like Woodvale, would end up as jet pilots. For example, they dispensed with the downwind and base leg calls, normally used by civilian pilots. Instead, once they had entered the circuit, their FINALS call was made when they were actually on the base leg position. In other words, their circuit pattern was oval in shape, rather than rectangular, compared to what I had been used to. All very enlightening, unless one had been trained in military procedures. As I hadn't had this privilege, I had to learn the hard way. In fact, control wise, the only thing I found in common with civil procedures, was in the taxiing, take-off and landing R/T terminology of control. Everything else was foreign to me.

To make matters more difficult, at least for me, was that two R/T frequency channels blasted out from the control desk loud speakers, they being VHF and UHF, depending upon the nature of a particular aircraft's detail and, to confuse the issue further, the type of aircraft flown! An interesting insight into the workings of a combined R.A.F. and civilian environment.

As it so happened, I only spent 5 months at Woodvale before returning, once again, to my old haunt Blackpool. Due to my infrequent attendance at Woodvale, I didn't get a chance to validate. Nevertheless, I was grateful to my employer at this aerodrome for giving me the chance to return to the world of ATC.

Before leaving there, it is perhaps worth mentioning that, apart from myself as an ex SATCO, another member of the controller staff, was Alec, ex- CAA chief officer at Liverpool airport who, in Preston Airways days, had been an 'A' man with me. I mention this purely as an indication that, despite our ages, we 'oldies' were still a force to be reckoned with!

My return to Blackpool was thanks to Mike, still in situ as Blackpool's SATCO, who indicated that if I was interested, the vacancy for a controller, that had cropped up in his section was mine for the asking. Once again, I could not believe my luck. Fate had played into my hands.

I left Woodvale at the end of January 1990 and started my second innings at Blackpool the very next day, February 1st.

I found myself being re-employed at the normal retirement age of 65 – how lucky can one get! Initially my re-instatement was for a six-month period, on what I thought would be a part time basis; at least that was what I was led to believe. No way, it soon became apparent that I would be fulfilling a permanent position and what's more the six-month deadline was extended time and again.

On reflection a perfect illustration of the old adage that one should never leave a job under a cloud, as you never know when an opportunity might arise whereby you would be welcomed back, as had happened to me. At my time of life, such philosophy was handsomely rewarded; my cup of fulfilment was overflowing.

My first stint back in the 'hot seat' at Blackpool was rewarded by a verbal 'welcome back' exchange over the R/T, by one of the flying club bosses, who was noted for his reservations about having an ATC service in the first place! One or two other pilots expressed similar sentiments whereby, if nothing else, it made me feel as though I was back where I belonged.

Whilst on the subject of non-standard verbal exchanges over our R/T frequency, the chi-chat between myself and our customers, did occasionally become rather personal, even embarrassing. An example of this non-standard R/T phraseology was when my son, a Captain with the resident airline, upon hearing my voice when I was controlling, would greet me with the words "Good morning/afternoon Dad" followed by equally non-standard R/T details of his intentions. Such conversations were not covered by the official CAA R/T phraseology publication! I, not to be out done, would reply in similar fashion. Whenever such 'exchanges' occurred, it caused no end of amusement to whoever was on duty with me at the time

The following is a classic example of the occasional use of non-standard R//T phraseology, which I resorted to on every occasion where an aircraft's characteristics warranted its use.

For example if I knew, or was pretty sure, an aircraft had a retractable undercarriage I always said "check your wheels down and locked".

On one particular occasion a controller, who shall remain nameless, cleared an aircraft to land without noticing that its wheels were still in the UP position, as a consequence of which the aircraft belly-landed. On asking the said controller why didn't he adopt my, admittedly, non-standard R/T advice, he simply replied " its not in the book"! I rest my case.

On two other occasions the following non-standard procedures occurred.

On the first one the well known legless fighter pilot, Douglas Bader, was instructed by me to taxi out and take-off on a particular runway. At the material time there was thick fog on the airfield, so much so that I couldn't see D.B.'s aircraft taxi out, let alone take-off. Subsequently I heard that he took off on another runway, not the one I thought he would use. On reflection, due to the weather conditions, I presume he thought it prudent to line up and take off on the first runway he came to whereby he could see the white centre-line markings. Not the first time my instructions were ignored!

The second time my instructions were ignored was the time when my first aviation employer, the renowned ex Pathfinder Chief AVM D. Bennett, landed on our one and only partly disused runway, due entirely to the strong wind direction along this particular runway, coupled with the type of light aircraft he was piloting whereby he really had no alternative but to do what he did.

Being an ex-aviator myself, unlike some of my compatriots, I tended to turn a blind eye to such flouting of ATC rules and regulations. As I've said before "Rules are for the guidance of wise men and the obedience of fools"!

Other flyers, who knew me of old, on hearing my voice, replied to my calls in similar vein. Strictly speaking, an initial call from an aircraft to ATC, should always be pre-fixed by the name of the station being called. For example, an aircraft calling us should say 'Blackpool this is ... (aircraft call-sign). Similarly, we, transmitting to an aircraft, pre-fixed such calls with the aircraft's call-sign, followed by this is 'Blackpool'. I cannot deny that standard R/T phraseology did, at times, degenerate which, for my sins, I was party to. Professionally, the only reservations I had to these unorthodox procedures, was that I invariably let those who made the initial R/T call, start the 'personal ball' rolling, before I replied in similar manner. I must emphasise though, that I only agreed to such practices under favourable weather conditions, and favourable traffic situations. If the 'chips' were down i.e. the weather factor and/or traffic density, was not conducive to light hearted radio banter, then there was no question but to return to authorised procedures. In my opinion such levity, provided it is not overdone, is a kind of safety valve in preventing tensions building up in, what is after all, a stressful occupation at times. The CAA would have had a field day if they had listened to our conversations. As noted earlier, all communications are taped, in the event of accident or incident investigations.

Changing the subject, the traffic mix of schedules, executives, helicopters, occasional military aircraft and of course, the predominant club/private flying activity had not changed all that much since my previous involvement. If anything, the latter activity showed no signs of abating.

To add interest to conventional ATC procedures, I now found myself involved in what I can only describe as 'out of the ordinary' controlling practices. They being types of aerial machines that I had not come across before. About 10 miles North of us there was an area in which microlight flying took place. In the early days they kept their activities to themselves, operating from a farmer's field. Later on they tended to spread their wings and paid us the odd visit. To begin with, they had no radio, so the first we knew about them was when they appeared in our circuit, mixing it with conventional flying machines. Then it was a question of, quickly out with the Aldis lamp, in the hope that they were familiar with light signals. Later on, most of them decided that it would be in their own interests to equip their machines with radio, so that they could be more easily be fitted in amongst our resident flyers. This, of course, suited us down to the ground. Microlights came in all shapes and sizes, some of which, looked distinctly Heath Robinson! They didn't appeal to me as a mode of transport, being very basic in design and construction, and wide open to the elements. Piloting these 'aircraft' was obviously an enthusiast's way of life.

Another unusual flying machine, if you can call them that, were the occasional visitation of the advertising airships, the Europa and the Orange. If I remember rightly we were given the opportunity of flying in them. Personally, again not a mode of transport I fancied, being enclosed in a gondola suspended beneath a huge envelope of helium gas. I must admit, when these impressive objects were on the ground, they were quite a spectacle. One could view them from all angles as they constantly weather cocked into wind when attached to their mooring masts. I was told that the pilot's cockpit was not dissimilar to that of a conventional airliner, being fully equipped with radio, nav: aids, instrumentation, etc. The engines that propelled these Goliath's were suitably placed adjacent the gondola cabin.

Both these airships, when moored for the night, glowed with their myriads of light bulbs shining their advertisement 'wares' and, during the annual Blackpool's Illuminations spectacular, gave the airport its own form of illuminations.

From a controlling exercise, there was little difference in the way we treated these airships. All we had to remember was that they could be a bit ungainly in strongish winds and, due to their low airspeed, they took time to depart/land and cross our airspace therefore due allowance had to be made of their progress, in relation to faster moving machinery.

As a memento of these visits I, and others in ATC, were presented with neckties imprinted with their respective logos.

Yet another unusual activity we experienced was in the sphere of Hot Air Balloon's, although none of them were based with us. Mainly in the summer months, they popped up at regular intervals, from the surrounding countryside. Some of them, but not all, carried radio, which I didn't think they would. I well remember one particular fine summer evening, when I was on duty. I happened to look out of the window when, lo and behold, first one of these contraptions rose majestically into the evening sky, followed by another and, yet another, until I counted no less than 12 of them proceeding sedately eastwards towards the Pennines. Where they eventually landed I have no idea. There were other occasions when at least half that number could be seen rising into the evening air. From our viewpoint there was no controlling involved, apart from warning powered aircraft of their presence.

Other aircraft of note that paid us visits were the following types.

An Arab Sheik, who was reputed to own a large slice of the Lake District, periodically called in, presumably to keep an eye on his property! For this purpose he owned, and used, a BAC 1-11 and a Boeing 707. The latter aircraft was surely an indication that we were no 'tiddler' sized aerodrome. We could easily accommodate the big ones. In fact, about the only large aircraft we couldn't entertain was the Jumbo Jet, (B.747) and Concorde, both of which would have rapidly run out of runway, if they tried to depart or land. Anyway, back to the Sheik's aircraft. I never saw the inside of these machines but, I was told, they were full of gold plate fittings and, the 707 was complete with an en-suite master bedroom; such opulence is hard to imagine! How the wealthy survive!

Twice during my latter stint at Blackpool, the British Open Golf Championship was held at Royal Lytham St Annes golf club, just down the road from us. Naturally for those golfers who owned their own aircraft, and quite a few of them did, they chose our airport to park their machines for the duration of the tournament. There was quite a variety of exotic machinery, one of which I particularly remember. I think it was a twin-engine Falcon type owned by Jack Nicklaus, complete with his personalised registration J I N, flown direct from the USA.

Whilst on the subject of this particular sporting event, it generated a lot of helicopter activity, taking players and officials to and from the golf course. More often than not, these 'choppers' flew through the take-off and landing paths of our regular customers which meant, whoever was controlling, had to have their wits about them.

In conclusion, that well known saying 'variety is the spice of life' was certainly an apt description of what went on at an airfield like ours. For my money, the infinitely variable 'menu' we faced, meant that there was never a dull moment in our controlling duties.

I cannot, in all honesty, claim that every day of the year, was a hive of activity. In deed, during the winter months and those days when the only things that flew were birds, meant a relaxation from the norm. To keep one mentally alert, the playing of cards and/or dominoes would keep us occupied. At least, that was my excuse for passing time!

One of the major changes I did come across was in the sphere of procedural control, which had been very much a part of my controlling duties, during my previous sojourn at Blackpool.

For instance, Warton subsequently enjoyed the advantage of having surveillance radar in which, part of its overall coverage, scanned the Irish Sea, where most of our commercial traffic operated. Due to the type of equipment they had, they were able to offer a Lower Airspace Radar Service (LARS) which could accommodate any traffic, not least ours. Our radar was not designed for such coverage and was, in any case, out of commission due to age. The assistance we got from Warton's radar facility did, to a large extent, do away from the procedural element of our controlling function. This helped us considerably and, at the same time, the commercial 'boys' appreciated the reduction in delays, inherent in procedural control. Furthermore, our colleagues at Warton, were always willing to assist us in resolving any tricky confliction problems that might arise. The only time we had to return to basic methods of control was weekends, bank holidays, etc., when Warton was closed.

Upon reaching my 65th birthday, there was still no sign of letting me off the hook, which, as far as I was concerned, suited me down to the ground.

Even my financial status took a distinct upward trend in my earnings as I now qualified for my 'bus pass', not forgetting the pension I had been receiving since my first retirement, my earnings took me into what I can only describe as a healthy income. I had never before enjoyed such financial rewards throughout my whole career. What I hadn't taken into account though was the taxman! His interest in my financial affairs had completely escaped my attention. Once he caught up with me I came down to earth with a bump. Notwithstanding the tax authorities, my additional earnings enabled me to invest in a Bungalow; something I had always dreamed about, as a retirement home now the family had fled the nest. My new homestead was nine miles from the airport in a quiet rural area.

I carried on full time employment for a couple of years but I have to admit I was beginning to tire of constant work attendance, presumably due, I suppose, to the inescapable fact of the ageing process. Nevertheless I was reluctant to give up altogether and if my new boss was prepared to use my services on a part time basis then I reckon I could cope. I was now at the mercy of another SATCO's decision as to my future. Mike Parkes had since left and joined the CAA. His successor was Dave Edmondson, an ex watch supervisor at Leeds Airport. I must have struck the right cord with him, albeit he had only witnessed my performance intermittently, as he acceded to my request without hesitation. So, until my final retirement in June 1995, that was how I was employed. In this last stage of my ATC career, I tended to look upon it as a kind of hobby, the beauty of which, I was being paid for it!

My involvement in the aviation scene had obviously rubbed off on my family. Apart from my son, who was one of the local airline's skippers, my daughter was invited to join the local handling agency Servisair, the largest company in this field of aviation enterprises.

The airport was becoming quite a family affair to the extent that some 'wags' suggested re-naming it 'Kilburn's Field'! Even my grandson Richard, my daughter's offspring not to be outdone, became a keen aircraft spotter, Blackpool being the ideal place for this kind of hobby. At the tender age of 13 he even had a trial flying lesson, thanks to yours truly winning this prize in the annual airport golf competition and, according to the instructor, he took to flying like a duck to water.

Time was now drawing near when I was 'persuaded' to relinquish my reigns and leave it to my off-spring to perpetuate the family name, where I had left off.

My second and final retirement party organised by my boss and my family, who kept me in the dark as to how they proposed to signal my departure from the aviation scene was some 'do'. It started off with Brian Bateson circling the party venue, in ever decreasing circles, at a very low height, towing a banner with the words "Well done John" written on it – an unexpected and much appreciated gesture from someone who normally charges the earth for such things. Mine was free.

I was amazed at the number of people who turned up to wish me 'bon voyage' which included some of those who retired with me on the first occasion. Some of my ATC colleagues even came from as far away as Bristol, London and those, nearer home, whom I only really knew by their voices over the telephone. Amongst the pilot fraternity there was one who remembered my passion for traditional jazz music and organised a live quartet to entertain the assembled gathering.

To cap it all, Dave the SATCO told all and sundry about my past, leaving out the juicier bits, reminiscent of the TV programme "This is your life". Most embarrassing I wished afterwards, purely as an ego trip, that somebody had recorded it!

Somewhere along the line, I must have struck the right chord in my relationships with work colleagues and the numerous aviation personalities I had come across during my career as a controller. On that note, I rest content on whatever laurels I may have possessed.

One final word I would like to pen, before I sign off for good.

I have always been a great believer that a controller's performance should, to a certain extent, be governed by practical application. By that I mean, applying common sense in his deliberations. Rules and regulations are, of course, necessary but they cannot legislate for every eventuality therefore the sentiment I have expressed is, in my opinion, an essential ingredient in a controller's make- up. I suspect most pilots would agree with me.

As I remarked at the beginning of this saga, I had had a very good innings in my chosen vocation in life. I would even go so far as to say that I was proud of having served in a profession, which I regarded as second to none.

I had spent my life in aviation since the tender age of 18. My working life covered a period of 52 years.

As a radio technician, my old friend Barry, having originally retired with me, first time round, said upon my second retirement party in September 1995.

"Are you making a habit of this John?"

C'est la vie!

~ END ~

My father with his miniature railway.

My Father's motor launch... but where was it?

No. 1 Air Crew Wing
"B" Squadron

No. 2 Radio School
X27 Unit Class "B"

Photograph by VIVIANS.

Cadets Brant Fearick Hiller Parker McMillan
Cadets Plant Farrand Mitchellhill Smart Sgt. Hirst Cadets Forsyth Sobel Reynolds Kilburn
Cadets Hardy Wyse Masson F/Lt F. D. Nicol Cadets Nairn Malone Quine

RAF training.

My Lancaster crew.

~ 188 ~

The Full Monty!

Ex-RAF Men For Korea?

Volunteers for Korea, all former RAF men, signing forms today in London's Brevet Flying Club, which has offered the Korean Minister in London a squadron of fighter pilots. Left to right (standing) are D. R. Cunningham, ex-W/O air gunner, of Cheam; and N. J. P. Kilburn, former Flight-Sergeant wireless operator. Sitting is R. M. Propert-Williams from South Wales. He was a F/O pilot.

A lucky escape!

Avro Tudor II and V

Avro York

H.P. Hermes

Vickers Viking

De Haviland DC3 Dakota

De Haviland DC4 Skymaster

Convair CV240

B170 Freighter

De Haviland Dove

The aircraft in which I flew as a Civil Aviation Radio Officer.

Drawings by the Author.

The Author and wife Bette depart Germany for the last time.

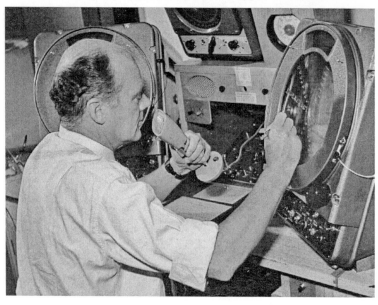

The Author at work with Radar set.